Domestic Violence

Cross Cultural Perspective

Domestic Violence
Cross Cultural Perspective

Edited by
M. Basheer Ahmed M.D.

Published for
MCC for Human Services, North Texas

To order additional copies of this book, contact:
Xlibris Corporation
1-888-795-4274
www.Xlibris.com
Orders@Xlibris.com
62894

Contents

Preface

M. Basheer Ahmed M.D.

D URING LATTER PART of 20 century there has been a massive influx of immigrants and refugees from Asia and Middle East to the United States. They brought with them a religion and a culture, which is different from the predominant Christian Western culture. In spite of this difference the incidence of Domestic Violence is similar among the immigrants as in the US. Helping the victims of Domestic Violence presents a challenging problem, for the professionals, educated and trained in United States, due to the lack of familiarity with Eastern religions and cultures. Many health professional who are managing shelters and helping victims of Domestic Violence are eager to learn the uniqueness of different religions and cultures of the victims of Domestic Violence whom they are helping.

Domestic violence is a global phenomenon occurring among people of all races, ages, social economic status, educational and religious backgrounds.

Family roles, values, customs and expectations are deeply rooted within a person's culture and religious traditions. As our society becomes increasingly multi-cultural, it is critical that we understand domestic violence within a cross-cultural context. Such an understanding will enable us to develop culturally appropriate interventions in addressing the issue of domestic violence in our communities. Culture includes values believes, customs, religions and social and interpersonal relationship which pass on from generation to generation. Cultural patterns by themselves do not cause domestic violence but certainly create an environment that foster and maintain conditions which promote domestic violence.

Professor Hernández in his opening chapter summarizes various topics discussed in the book related to psychodynamics of abuse and cross-cultural, Islamic, Jewish and Hindu perspective. The other topics covered are effects of domestic violence on children and the legal aspects of domestic violence. The last chapter gives a detailed description of the development of a domestic violence program for the immigrant communities from South Asia, Middle East and Africa.

This book is written for health professionals, religious and community leaders to make them familiar with some unique feature of people following different religions and cultures. The book addresses the aspects of domestic violence from different cultural and religious orientations and suggests strategies to help victims and perpetrators. This book is written in a simple language to be easily understood by professionals, para-professionals, religious and community leaders, who can play a significant role in treating and preventing domestic violence in the community.

Acknowledgements

I would like to thank Professor Santos Hernández, Dr. Najma Adam, Dr. Zainab Alwani, Dr. Toby Myers, Ms. Avayam Ramani, Ms. Rosalyn Hubbard, Ms. Erin Hendricks and Ms. Talaun Thompson for their unique contributions, and MCC for Human Services, North Texas, Tarrant County Medical Society, United Way of Tarrant County, Multi-cultural Alliance, Darul Eman Educational Center, Al Hedayah Islamic School and Islamic Association of Carrollton and Islamic Association of Collin county for their encouragement and support for publishing this book.

M. Basheer Ahmed. M.D.
July, 2009 Arlington, TX USA

Contributors

Santos H. Hernández, Ph.D., L.M.S.W-A.P.

Dr. Hernández received a Bachelor of Arts degree and a Master of Social Work degree from Our Lady of the Lake University of San Antonio. He received a Ph.D. in Social Work from the University of Denver.

Dr. Hernández has been a social work educator for over thirty-three years. From 1998-2008, he served as Dean of the School of Social Work at the University of Texas, Arlington (UTA). Prior to joining UTA, he was Dean of the Worden School of Social Service at Our Lady of the Lake University. He previously served on the faculties of California State University, Fresno, the University of Denver, Eastern Washington University and San Jose State University.

Dr. Hernández has published, taught and done research in the areas of cross cultural social work practice, mental health, and generalist social work practice.

He co-authored a social work practice text *The Integration of Social Work Practice* (1995) and co-edited an international text *La Familia en América Del Norte: Evolución, problemática and política* (2002) and several articles and book chapters.

He is currently working on a text, *Skills and Competencies in Human Services Administration: Toward An Evidence-Based Approach* under contract with Eddie Bowers Publishing. He serves on the editorial boards of *Research on Social Work Practice;* the *Journal of Baccalaureate Social Work; and, Social Work Education.*

He has been involved in a broad cross section of community and professional activities. He currently serves on the board for SafeHaven Women's Shelter of Tarrant County and the Community Services Division Cabinet of the United Way of Metropolitan Tarrant County.

M. Basheer Ahmed M.D.

Dr. Basheer Ahmed was born in Hyderabad (DN), India. He graduated with a degree in biological sciences from Osmania University in Hyderabad, India and obtained medical degree from Dow Medical College, Karachi,

Pakistan. He completed his postgraduate studies in psychiatry at Glasgow University, Scotland. He was elected as Fellow of the Royal College of Physicians, Canada (FRCP) in 1975 and was elected fellow of the Royal college of Psychiatrists, London in 1981. He is a Board Certified Psychiatrist and he is a distinguished life fellow of the American Psychiatric Association. He held the positions of Assistant Professor of Psychiatry at Albert Einstein College of Medicine in New York, Professor of Psychiatry at Wright State University Medical School Dayton, Ohio and Professor of Psychiatry at Southwestern Medical School, Dallas, Texas. He is currently in private practice in Fort Worth, Texas.

Dr. Ahmed is the member of Tarrant County Medical Society and Texas Medical Association. He is the past president of the Tarrant Chapter of Texas Psychiatrist Society. He is the past president of Islamic Association of Tarrant County, past president of the Islamic Medical Association of North America. He is the former member of Board of Directors, Islamic Social Service Association of North America. He is a member of Board of Directors of the Multi Cultural Alliance of North Texas. He is a founding member and President of Institute of Medieval and Post-Medieval studies of North Texas. He has presented numerous papers nationally and internationally. He has organized conferences on Domestic Violence—Islamic Perspective and Cross Cultural Perspective. He has also published numerous articles in various professional journals. **His recent article on "Domestic Violence, the responsibilities of physicians, health care providers and community leaders" appeared in Tarrant County Physician Journal in May 2008.** He recently edited two books "Muslim Contribution to World Civilization" published by International Institute of Islamic Thought—Virginia, "Islamic Intellectual Heritage And It's Impact on the West" Published by Institute of Medieval and Post Medieval Studies—North Texas.

Dr. Ahmed is the founder and chairman of the **Muslim Community Center for Human Services**, which is a medical, and a social service organization, helping indigents residing in Dallas Fort Worth area. The MCC for Human Services offers free medical services to indigent residents of the Dallas/Ft. Worth areas irrespective of color, ethnicity, or religion. It also offers counseling services to clients with marital problems, emotional disturbance, and victims of domestic violence. MCC has received small grants from Foundation of Community Empowerment, Dallas, Texas and U.S. Department of Justice to develop volunteer training for Domestic

Violence Program. Dr. Ahmed has received the Tarrant County Medical Society 2008 Physician Humanitarian Award January 25th 2008.

Najma M. Adam, Ph.D.

Dr. Adam completed her Ph.D. in Social Work from Jane Addams College of Social Work at the University of Illinois in Chicago, and her Master of Arts from the School of Social Service Administration at the University of Chicago.

She held several academic positions and is currently an Associate Professor, Social Work Department, College of Health and Human Services, Governors State University, University Park, Illinois. Her dissertation work and subsequent research has focused on domestic violence in the South Asian Community. She has published on this social problem and has presented extensively both nationally and internationally. Her teaching areas are domestic violence, research methods, social policy, and women's studies.

Zainab Alwani, Ph.D

Dr. Alwani received her Ph.D. in Islamic Sciences (Fiqh and Usul Al-Fiqh) Islamic Jurisprudence, from the International Islamic University in Malaysia. She is currently the Program Director and an Adjunct Professor of Arabic Language Studies at Northern Virginia Community College. She also teaches Arabic Studies at the School of Advanced International Studies at Johns Hopkins University, where she developed courses in Arabic Studies that focus on the link between Islamic philosophy, language and culture. She is also a professor at a number of consortium institutions including Wesley Theological Seminary, the Washington National Cathedral and Cordoba University.

As an educator, Dr. Alwani brings over 15 years of teaching and curriculum development experience in Islamic and Arabic Studies. She is as a researcher, social and community activist, she's the first female Jurist on the Fiqh council of North America. She is also a board member of KARAMAH: Muslim Women Lawyers for Human Rights, Washington, DC. And the Foundation for Appropriate and Immediate Temporary Help, a community based organization in Herndon, Virginia, and an Executive Member of the Fiqh Council of North America.

She has devoted herself to numerous activities; she has presented and lectured at numerous conferences, workshops and events, involving: Islamic history, Islamic culture and jurisprudence, conflict resolution, contemporary Muslim women's and family issues, domestic violence, and female empowerment in American Muslim communities.

Dr. Alwani has co-authored a number of books which include, Change from within: a Diverse Perspectives on Domestic Violence in Muslim Communities, and What Islam Says about Domestic Violence. Perspectives: Arabic language and culture in films, Published by Alucen Learning, USA.

She has also published a variety of scholarly articles on the topics of Fiqh legislation, Maqasid Al shariah, Peace Jihad and Conflict Resolution in America, Al ghazali and his Methodology, Aisha's "*Istidrakat*" Commentaries and the Methodological Premises: Reclaiming a Lost Legacy, in renowned publications including Islamiyat Alma'rafa published by the International Institute of Islamic Thought; the American Journal of Islamic and Social Sciences published by the Association of Muslim Social Scientists; the journal of Women and Civilization published by the Association for the study of Women in Civilization.

In addition to her academic and social activities Dr. Alwani is also an active member of the American Council on the Teaching of Foreign Languages (ACTFL), Association for Supervision and Curriculum Development (ASCD), The American Association of Teachers of Arabic (AATA), The Abrahamic Roundtable at the Washington National Cathedral, the Woman's Faith and Development Alliance (WFDA), and the Middle East Studies Association (MESA).

She has received Awarded Who's Who among America's Teachers for three consecutive years during 2003-2006. She has also received an award for her community activism from the University of Texas for contributing to research on domestic violence from a cross cultural perspective.

Toby Myers, Ed.D.

A longtime worker in the Battered Women's Movement, Toby Myers helped to found the first shelter in Houston, TX. She was one of the original organizers of the Texas Council on Family Violence, the first board chair, and served 20 years on the board. A founding board member of the National

Center on Domestic and Sexual violence, Myers is Board Vice-President. She served on the Jewish Advisory Committee of the Faith Trust Institute formerly Center for the Prevention of Sexual and Domestic Violence. Serving on the Steering Committee of the National Coalition Against Domestic Violence and chairing the Family Violence Advisory Committee for the Texas Department of Human Services, Myers was one of the 150 appointees by then Surgeon General C. Everett Koop to his policy making group on Violence and Public Health.

Her research has been published in domestic and international journals and she served on the editorial boards of Violence against Women and Religion and Abuse. She is a Licensed Professional Counselor and a Licensed Clinical Social Worker. Myers has held a faculty post at Texas Woman's University and adjunct positions at the University of Texas Health Science Center at Houston-School of Public Health and at University of Houston Clear Lake. She developed and taught what is thought to be the first graduate course in domestic violence in Texas. She is recognized as an Expert Witness in domestic violence cases.

Referred to as "the mother of the Texas Battered Women's Movement" by the Texas Council on Family Violence, Toby Myers helped found and has been active in many organizations to end violence against women. Her domestic violence related activities include work with attorneys as an expert witness, a counseling practice, serving on boards and committees, training, and technical assistance. A good friend of gray hair, crow's feet, and cellulite, Myers dreams of people living in intimate relationships not only non-violent, but also mutually respectful, mutually satisfying, and growth promoting.

Avayam Ramani, L.M.S.W.

Ms. Ramani completed her degree in social work from the State University of Madras, India and has been working with Parkland Health and Hospital System as a social worker for twenty years. Her responsibilities include discharge-planning, education, information referrals, service coordination and follow-ups. She does volunteer work with domestic violence programs focusing on immigrants from South Asia, especially from India. She has a special interest in studying the influence of religion and or culture that may precipitate abusive behavior towards women.

DOMESTIC VIOLENCE CROSS CULTURAL PERSPECTIVE

Rosalyn Hubbard, M.S.S.W.

Ms. Hubbard completed her undergraduate studies in criminal justice and social work and obtained her masters in social work from the University of Texas at Arlington. She has eleven years experience with the Texas Department of Family and Protective Services. She has served in many capacities to include an Investigative Supervisor, Domestic Violence Liaison and currently as the Regional Substance Abuse Specialist. She has investigated a number of children raised in an abusive environment. Her interest on the effect of abusive behavior on children was a result from her personal experiences in handling these cases. She has association with many professional organizations including Health Marriage Healthy Family Coalition of Tarrant County and Tarrant County Council on Family Violence.

Erin Hendricks, J.D.D.A

Erin Hendricks is an Assistant District Attorney with the Dallas County District Attorney's Office. Erin is the chief prosecutor assigned to the County's first Sexual Assault Prosecution Unit. She worked in the Family Violence Felony Division for five years and was formerly assigned as felony supervisor to the Family Violence Misdemeanor Section.

Originally from Fort Worth, Erin received a Bachelor's degree in Spanish from the University of Texas Austin. She started at the D.A.'s office in the summer of 2002 after graduating from the Dedman School of Law School at SMU. While at SMU, she was a student director for the law school's Domestic Violence Symposium.

Erin has presented on issues of family violence prosecution to students, advocates and social workers, law enforcement officials, medical providers, judges and other prosecutors at conferences and trainings across Texas. Outside of the courthouse, Erin serves on the Board of Directors for the Genesis Women's Shelter auxiliary group "Shareholders." She is committed to providing help and services to victims of domestic and sexual violence and increasing the community's knowledge of the reality and prevalence of violence against women.

Talaun Thompson, L.M.S.W.

Ms. Thompson completed her undergraduate degree in Psychology and her graduate studies in Sociology and Social work from the University of

Texas at Arlington. She is a Ph.D. candidate completing her doctoral studies in Psychology at Capella University, Minneapolis, MN.

Ms. Thompson is a licensed Social Worker and has previously worked as a medical social worker and a mental health substance abuse counselor. She has been the Program Director for Muslim Community Center for Human Services since 2006 and has a major responsibility for the domestic violence program of the center.

Ms. Thompson is a member of the National Association of Social Workers, the International Sociology Honor Society and the International Association for Applied Psychology.

She has engaged in international research and received the West African fellowship from the University of Texas at Arlington. She has presented papers at various conferences and seminars and her research interests include interpersonal perceptions, attachment theory and marital discord particularly as it relates to issues of violence against women.

Domestic Violence; It's EVERYBODY'S Business!

Santos H. Hernández, Ph.D., L.M.S.W.-A.P.

THE BANNER ON the website of the Oakland County Coordinating Council Against Domestic Violence reads, *"Domestic Violence; It's EVERYBODY'S Business! Domestic violence should not happen to anybody. Ever. Period!"*. While domestic violence should not happen to anyone, unfortunately it does happen, and it could potentially happen to anyone. Domestic violence is both a national and a worldwide crisis. According to a 2000 UNICEF study, *20-50%* of the female population of the world will become the victims of domestic violence. (Kapoor, 2000). Within the United States, one out of every four American women will experience violence by an intimate partner sometime during her lifetime. One out of every six women will be raped during her lifetime. (Tjaden & Thoennes, 1999).

At a recent event held by a local women's shelter to highlight men's legacy in fighting domestic violence, the keynote speaker, former professional football player, Don McPherson, emphasized that domestic violence is not just a women's issue, it is a men's issue. By viewing domestic violence only as a women's issue men are all too often absolved from having to address the problem. In reality, since an overwhelming percent of domestic violence, some say over 90%, is perpetrated by men against women, we have to see this as a men's issue. McPherson called for men to become more aware of how they use violence and their attitudes toward women to reinforce their sense of maleness. He argued that this limits men in that it does not permit them to become a "whole person". Persons who are whole do not define themselves in relation to others, do not need to demean or dominate others and are not limited in their expression of sensitivities and vulnerabilities. Until men can become "whole persons" and teach their sons to be "whole persons" we will continue to experience domestic violence and other exploitations of women.

Attitudes toward domestic violence even by human service professions have evolved dramatically over the past thirty years. In the 1970s and 1980s, domestic violence was seen as rooted in poor relationship choices made by women. Interventions often focused on helping the women develop better relationship skills. Law enforcement was hesitant to intervene or even respond to domestic disturbance calls citing that these were among the most dangerous of all calls for assistance. More often than not, law enforcement also reflected the bias that domestic disturbances were protected by the sanctity of marriage. Ultimately, few calls for assistance resulted in the removal of the perpetuator. Even the mental health system was conspiratorial in that battered women were often diagnosed with adjustment disorders in order to receive services. Fortunately, contemporary views of domestic violence have changed such that victims, while still experiencing difficulty, are less prone to being stigmatized. Our knowledge of domestic violence and effective interventions has made us more aware of the complicity of dynamics involved in family violence. Laws have changed to afford victims greater tools to combat the effects of family violence and communities have increasingly realized that effective interventions must be community based. We now understand that we don't have a problem with domestic violence because women make poor choices, but rather because violence has become a problem in our society.

As we learned more about domestic violence, we developed a broader understanding of the cultural dimensions of the problem. Studies have found that effective interventions take into account culture (Hancock & Siu, 2009; Montalvo-Liendo, 2009; Tehee, & Esqueda, 2008; Yick, & Oomen-Early, 2008) and religious beliefs (Wendt, 2008) and involve community based interventions (Malik, Ward, & Janczewski, 2008) and collaborations across service sectors. (Buchbinder & Eisikovits, 2008).

Domestic violence is a matter of exploitation and domination. The Office of Violence Against Women defines domestic violence as a pattern of coercive controls that one person exercises over another. It involves physical, emotional, verbal and sexual abuse and stalking. Stalking is repeated harassment that makes the victim feel scared or upset. A stalker can be someone known to the victim or a stranger. They often bother people by giving them attention they do not want. Stalking is serious, it is against the law, and often turns to physical violence.

Domestic violence is behavior that physically harms, arouses fear, prevents victims from doing what they wish or forces them to behave in ways they do not want. It includes the use of physical and sexual violence, threats and intimidation, emotional abuse and economic deprivation.

Domestic violence and emotional abuse are behaviors used by one person in a relationship to control the other. (domesticviolence.org) Domestic violence can happen to anyone of any race, age, sexual orientation, religion or gender. It can happen to couples who are married, living together or who are dating. Domestic violence affects people of all socioeconomic backgrounds and education levels. Domestic violence occurs across the world, in various cultures, (Watts & Zimmerman, 2002) and affects people across society, irrespective of economic status. (Waits, 1985). In the *United States*, according to the Bureau of Justice Statistics women are about six times as likely as men to experience intimate partner violence. (Bachman & Saltzman, 1995)

Although both men and women can be abused, most victims are women. Children in homes where there is domestic violence are more likely to be abused and/or neglected. Most children in these homes know about the violence. Even if a child is not physically harmed, they may have emotional and behavior problems. (domesticviolence.org)

While there are many theories regarding domestic abuse, domestic violence advocates have increasingly argued that abuse is not an accident. They see abuse is an intentional act that one person uses in a relationship to control the other. Abusers have learned to abuse so that they can get what they want. (domesticviolence.org)

On it's *Did You Know?* webpage, SafeHaven of Tarrant County presents the following statistics regarding the prevalence of domestic violence:

1 in 3 women have been victims of domestic violence at some point during their lives. *Journal of American Medical Association, 2001*

On average, more than 3 women are murdered by their intimate partners in the United States every day. *The United States Department of Justice, 2001*

Each day in the United States, more than 3 children die as a result of abuse at home. *The United States Department of Health and Human Services, 2001*

As many as 10 million children witness domestic violence each year in the U.S. *Texas Council on Family Violence, 2003*

A child's exposure to the father abusing the mother is the strongest risk factor for transmitting violent behavior from one generation to the next. *The American Psychological Association, 1996*

1 in 5 high school aged girls will be physically and/or sexually abused in a dating relationship, increasing the likelihood that the girl will abuse drugs and/or alcohol, develop an eating disorder, consider and/or attempt suicide, engage in risky behavior and/or become pregnant. *The Journal of the American Medical Association, 2001*

Over 324,000 pregnant women are involved in abusive relationships each year. *The Maternal and Child Health Journal, 2000*

An abuser's unemployment, access to guns and threats of deadly violence are the strongest warning signs of female homicide in abusive relationships. *The American Journal of Public Health, 2003*

The health-related costs of rape, physical assault, stalking and homicide committed by intimate partners is more than $5.8 billion each year. *The Centers for Disease Control and Prevention, 2003 http://www.safehaventc. org/content/did_you_know.html*

As the webpage for DomesticViolence.Org, quoted at the begining of this discussion, says: ANYONE CAN BE VICTIM! Domestic Violence is an epidemic that crosses all demographic, social, and educational boundaries.

Organization of this book.

The remaining seven articles in this book are distinct but interrelated. They were presented at the *Second Regional Cross Cultural Conference on Domestic Violence* and address critical aspects of domestic violence from various cultural and religious perspectives.

In *Domestic Violence Introduction and Overview*, conference organizer and Muslin Community Center for Human Services Executive Director, M. Basheer Ahmed, M.D., overviews the dynamics of abuse and the cycle of violence. He discusses the prevalence of domestic violence as a universal problem within various religious and population groups. Dr. Ahmed then discusses prevention strategies involving community programs, religious leaders and the role of the father in teaching boys about the expression of anger without the use of violence.

In *Domestic Violence: Cross-Cultural Perspective, The Power of One*, Najma M. Adam, Ph.D. discusses the power of the individual in countering cultural beliefs that contribute to domestic violence. No culture nor religious group is immune from this social problem. While culture provides us a sense of belonging, acceptance, and comfort as it makes and shapes us, cultural influences are often the culprit contributing to domestic violence against women. Dr. Adam argues that from the micro-perspective in how we parent and in how we manifest cultural beliefs, the individual has the POWER OF ONE and can make a difference in addressing ethnic-cultural practices that serve as an excuse for domestic violence and move us to greater ideals of social justice.

Family Relations: Islamic Perspective by Zainab Alwani discusses the Quran as emphasizing that all people, including women, are created equal in worth and value. In so doing, given the times, the Quran revolutionized the status of women in Islamic countries. He discusses particularly three points of misinterpretation of Verse 4:34 in regards to the use of the term, *daraba*. He then discusses domestic violence in the modern context and presents the Quran as providing a comprehensive model to protect the human family from oppression.

In *Jewish Perspectives in Domestic Violence*, Dr. Toby Myers discusses aspects of Judaism with regard to domestic violence. She notes that victims draw comfort, encouragement, and support from their Judaism and discusses prominent Jewish women's organizations and individuals that have worked to eliminate domestic violence. She concludes her discussion by presenting ways that Jews experiencing domestic violence have used rituals and prayers to alleviate their distress.

Avayam Ramani introduces us to Sashi in *The Hindu/Indian Woman and Domestic Violence*. Sashi struggles with her duty as a wife and mother and abuse from her husband. She sees her plight as karma and tells her friend that, "As a Hindu woman, I should follow a wife's dharma [duty]." Ramani presents a brief explanation of Indian culture and Hinduism with a discussion of vedas, upanisads, dharma, karma and reincarnation. Ramani notes that many Hindu women continue to suffer abuse in silence in the name of dharma and karma due to their misconceptions about Hindu teaching. Ramani concludes by exhorting Hindu women to become aware the changes brought about as a result of social activists' efforts to fight for women's rights and to take advance of programs and services aimed at protecting them from abuse.

Rosalyn Hubbard discusses *The Effects of Domestic Violence on Children.* She notes that studies have validated that there is a significant correlation between child and domestic abuse with serious consequences for the safety and emotional development of children. In discussing domestic violence witnessed by children, Hubbard notes that research suggests that between 80 and 90 percent of children in families experiencing domestic violence are aware of the violence. The resulting effect of this is that exposure to domestic violence increases the chance of the children being abused themselves. Studies have also indicated that adults who witnessed violence as children were significantly more likely to be involved in abuse relationships. She concludes her discussion by providing information for reporting domestic violence in Texas and other states.

In *An Introduction to Family Violence Prosecution with Consideration of the Diverse Victim Population* Erin Hendricks, Prosecutor for the Dallas County District Attorney's Office, discusses family violence as defined by the Texas Family Code and various legal recourses available to victims. Hendricks posits that the State prosecutes offenders on behalf of the victim, even if it may be against the wishes of the victim, in order to protect the victim, the children, and the community. The role of advocate in the criminal justice system is presented as bridging the gap between the victim and the prosecutor, helping each get the information she needs. Hendricks discusses various types of protective orders as safety tools used in family violence cases. The discussion overviews special circumstances presented by diverse populations based on culture, religion and immigrant status. It concludes with a quick reference guide to laws pertain to domestic violence situation.

Roshni (Domestic Violence Program in North Texas): Helping South Asian, Middle Eastern and African Immigrant Communities presents a discussion by Dr. M. Basheer Ahmed and Ms. Talaun Thompson regarding community programs offered by the Muslim Community Center for Human Services in responding to the needs of the immigrant community, particularly in relation to domestic violence. In addressing matters of domestic violence, Ahmed and Thompson state that knowledge, organization and the need for professional staff are essential components. In discussing Islam and domestic violence, they argue that studies of the Qu'ran, Hadith and Sunah have found that Islam does not endorse any type of violence or abuse. Because of the particular circumstances presented by culture, religion, and immigration status, the availability of a Muslim organization offering domestic violence programs and services helps alleviate some of the fears that a person might experience when approaching a mainstream agency. The Roshni (meaning light in Urdu language) Program is described as just such a program. The program's main objective is to promote healthy and harmonious family relationships in the Asian, Middle Eastern, and African immigrant communities.

Taken together, the chapters in this book address critical aspects of understanding domestic violence from a multi-cultural perspective, particularly as they affect ethnic-cultural and religious populations. Human service workers working with victims and perpetuators of domestic violence will find insightful information and resources within this book.

References Cited

Bachman, R.& Saltzman, L. E. (August 1995) (PDFNCJ 154348). *Violence against Women: Estimates from the Redesigned Survey.* Bureau of Justice Statistics. *http://www.ojp.usdoj.gov/bjs/pub/pdf/femvied.pdf*

Buchbinder, E. & Eisikovits, Z. (2008). Collaborative Discourse: The Case of Police and Social Work Relationships in Intimate Violence Intervention in Israel. *Journal of Social Service Research*, Vol. 34(4). Available online at *http://www.haworthpress.com*. C_ 2008 by The Haworth Press.

Hancock, T. U. & Siu, K. (2009). A Culturally Sensitive Intervention with Domestically Violent Latino Immigrant Men. *Journal of Family Violence.*24:123-132. DOI 10.1007/s10896-008-9217-0

Kapoor, Sushma. (June, 2000). Domestic Violence Against Women and Girls. UNICEF: Innocenti Research Centre. Cited by Feminist Majority Foundation. Domestic Violence Facts. *http://feminist.org/other/dv/dvfact. html#notes*

Malik, N.M., Ward, K. and Janczewski, C. (2008) Coordinated Community Response to Family Violence: The Role of Domestic Violence Service Organizations. *Journal of Interpersonal Violence* 2008; 23; 933 originally published online Mar 31, 2008.

Montalvo-Liendo, N. (2009) Cross-cultural factors in disclosure of intimate partner violence: an integrated review. *Journal of Advanced Nursing* 65(1), 20-34 doi: 10.1111/j.1365-2648.2008.04850.x

Tehee, M. & Willis Esqueda, C (2008). American Indian and European American Women's Perceptions of Domestic Violence. *Journal of Family Violence.* 23:25-35. DOI 10.1007/s10896-007-9126-7

Tjaden, P. & Thoennes, N. (1999). *Prevalence, Incidence, and Consequences of Violence Against Women: Findings from the National Violence Against Women Survey.* National Institute of Justice and Centers for Disease Control, Washington, DC (NIJ Grant #93-IJ-CX-0012). Available from the *US Department of Justice's Violence Against Women Office.*

U.S. Department of Justice. Office on Violence Against Women. About Domestic Violence. *http://www.usdoj.gov/ovw/domviolence.htm.*

Waits, K. (1985). The Criminal Justice System's Response to Battering: Understanding the Problem, Forging the Solutions. *Washington Law Review* 60: 267-330.

Watts C & Zimmerman C (April 2002). Violence against women: global scope and magnitude. *Lancet* 359 (9313): 1232-7. *doi:10.1016/ S0140-6736(02)08221-1. PMID 11955557.*

Wendt, S.(2008) Christianity and Domestic Violence: Feminist Poststructuralist Perspectives. *Affilia*; 23; 144.

Yick, A. G. and Oomen-Early, J. (2008). A 16-Year Examination of Domestic Violence Among Asians and Asian Americans in the Empirical Knowledge Base: A Content Analysis. *Journal of Interpersonal Violence.* 23; 1075 originally published online Feb 7, 2008.

Resources for Additional Information

Domestic Violence.Org
http://www.domesticviolence.org/

Domestic Violence Information Center
http://feminist.org/other/dv/dvhome.html

Medline Plus, Domestic Violence
http://www.nlm.nih.gov/medlineplus/domesticviolence.html

National Domestic Violence Hotline
http://www.ndvh.org/

SafeHaven of Tarrant County:
http://www.safehaventc.org/index.html

Domestic Violence: Psychodynamics and Prevention

M. Basheer Ahmed, M.D.

Introduction

IN THIS MOST civilized part of the world, it is sad to see the prevalence of the most uncivilized act, namely family violence. Every few seconds a woman is battered, a child is abused, or an elderly person is assaulted by his/her spouse, parents, or children. The home is supposed to be a safe place characterized by equality and partnership between the two spouses and a loving and nurturing environment for children and seniors.

Domestic violence is defined as a pattern of behavior occurring between two people who are or were in an intimate relationship (wife and ex-wife) with the intent to achieve control and dominance through emotional, psychological, physical, and sexual mistreatment (Flit Craft, Hadley, Hendricks et al, 1992). Such abusive behavior includes emotional and psychological abuse, as well as sexual and physical assault. Emotional abuse is characterized by cursing, screaming, and degradation of the other by constantly criticizing the spouse's thoughts, feelings, and opinions. Psychological abuse consists of threatening bodily harm, taking away the children, and killing the spouse or himself/herself. The perpetrator also controls the finances, food, and medication and places restrictions on socialization even with other family members. Physical abuse occurs when perpetrators actually hit, kick, punch, choke, or burn to such a degree that lacerations and fractures occur. Forcing unwanted sexual activity is also a form of sexual abuse.

Four million women are assaulted each year, making assault a leading cause of death and disability to women aged 15-44 in the United States (Greenfeld, 1998). Every day in this country, three women are murdered by their husbands or boyfriends. In 2000, 1,247 American women were killed by an intimate partner (Rennison, 2003). Thus, the number of women who were murdered by their spouses or boyfriends during 2003-08 may have exceeded the number of all American soldiers killed in Iraq since the invasion. One in every four women will experience domestic violence in her lifetime in United States.

While women are less likely than men to be victims of violent crimes overall, they are five to eight times more likely than men to be victimized by an intimate partner (Greenfeld, 1998). Thirty-seven percent of women sought treatment in emergency rooms for violence inflicted upon them by their intimate partners (Rennison, 2003). In Texas, there were 187,811 incidents of family violence in 2005, and over 12,000 women were living in domestic violence shelters in 2006 ("Texas Council on Family Violence," *The River,* 2007). Battered women have more than twice the health care needs and costs than those who are never battered. Approximately 17 percent of pregnant women report having been battered, which leads to miscarriages, stillbirths, and a two to four times greater likelihood of bearing a low-birth-weight baby (McFarlane et. al, 1992).

Significant numbers of homeless women have a history of domestic violence and mental health problems are common among the victims of domestic violence. Fifty-six percent of women who experience any partner violence are diagnosed with a psychiatric disorder, and 29% of all women who attempt suicide were battered. 37% of battered women have symptoms of depression, 46% have symptoms of anxiety disorder, and 45% experience Post Traumatic Stress Disorder (PTSD) (Danielson et. al, 1998). In the United States, the health care cost of intimate partner violence against women totals $5.8 billion each year (National Center for Injury Prevention and Control, 2003).

Many perpetrators use the work place to express their anger and harassment as well as to intimidate the spouse, ex-spouse, or girl friend. Every year, 18,000 incidents of such harassment are reported by a spouse or a former spouse (Duhart, 2001). In addition, an increasing number of reports are being published about young women experiencing violence at the hand of their boyfriends. Approximately one in five female high school students report being physically and/or sexually abused by a dating partner (Silverman, Raj et. al, 2001). Eight percent of high school aged girls said "yes" when asked if "a boyfriend or date has ever forced sex against your will."(Schoen, C., Davis, K. et. al, 1997). Forty percent of girls aged 14 to 17 reports knowing someone their age who has been hit or beaten by a boyfriend (Children Now/Kaiser Permanente poll, 1995).

Domestic violence may be passed onto children as a standard of behavior to be expected in intimate relationships. Children who witness violence against their mothers become emotionally distressed and, as a result, manifest childhood behavior problems and poor academic performance (Jaffe, P. and Suderman, M., 1995). Boys become violent themselves as adults, and girls will not identify violence as abusive and may accept abuse in their adult life as normal. A recent study of low-income pre-school children in Michigan found that nearly half (46.7 percent) of them had been exposed to at least one incident of mild or severe violence in the family. They suffered such PTSD symptoms as bed-wetting or nightmares, and were at greater risk than their peers of having allergies, asthma, gastrointestinal problems, and headaches (Graham-Bermann, S. and Seng, J., 2005). In a national survey of 600 American families, 50 percent of men who assaulted their wives frequently assaulted their children (Strauss, M.A., Gelles, R.J. et. al 1990).

Dynamics of an abusive relationship

Although there are rare cases of women who assault their husbands, by and large spousal abuse occurs because men batter women and get away with it. No single theory for why men show such aggressive behavior has been confirmed. While there are sex-linked differences that associate aggression and the male gender, but environmental and cultural factors play a significant role in developing this behavior. Abusive men come from a variety of backgrounds, religions, races, and occupations. Rigid sex role stereotypes are pervasive, as abusive men attempt to place their partners in a submissive role. Most of the abusers learned this behavior through life experiences in their own family and by observing society at large. They believe that they have the right to control others' behaviors, an idea that may be reinforced by their religious belief that a wife should be obedient and subservient. Such behavior is further reinforced when family members and religious organizations do not intervene, saying that it is a "private matter."

It has been noted that abusers are insecure, jealous, possessive, and emotionally dependent upon their partners. They usually have a history of battering, using force during arguments, breaking objects, showing cruelty toward children and animals (Harway, N. and Hansen, M., 1994). They justify their behavior and minimize its seriousness by saying that this happens in every marriage. Sometimes they blame their spouses for instigating the incident, which then forces them to resort to physical discipline. They avoid any guilt or shame that would make them feel bad by denying the entire incident, which is the abuser's most common defense mechanism (Ordona, T., 1995). Contrary to the general public's perception, most abusers have a good status in the community, may have a stable work record, and appear to be caring family men.

There is no specific psychological or cultural profile of an abused woman. These women often develop strong emotional ties with the perpetrator, due to the power imbalance between the two parties and because the treatment is intermittently good and bad. Dutton call this "traumatic bonding." A significant factor here is the intermittent and unpredictable abuse. While this may sound counterintuitive, the abuse is offset by an increase in positive behavior, such as attention, gifts, and promises. The abused individual also feels relief that the abuse has ended. Thus, there is intermittent reinforcement for the behavior, which is difficult to extinguish and instead serves to strengthen the bond between the abuser and the individual being abused (Dutton, D.G. and Painter, S.L., 1981).

Other factors for remaining within an abusive relationship are related to environmental influences. One frequently sees that an abused woman has been raised in an abusive environment and therefore accepts it as a normal behavior. Women who do not have enough confidence to stand on their own feet are easily subjected to the abuse. They are socially isolated and do not have family or community support. Some believe that accepting the violence will ultimately lead to a long-term resolution. Women who are constantly subjected to intimidation, humiliation, social isolation, accusation, and criticism are bound to develop low self-esteem, poor self-confidence, and poor ego strength. Some family members, elders, and religious leaders may even make them believe that they bring such abuse upon themselves due to their "provocative" behavior, and many victims do end up blaming themselves for their husbands' behavior.

Consequences of violence on victims

In a normal non-violent family, one sees equality and partnership. For example, decisions on important financial matters and household responsibilities are made jointly, each person's opinion is respected, and differences of opinion are handled with a compromising attitude that satisfies each partner. Unfortunately, the same is not true in an abusive relationship, where dominance and control are the major dynamics.

Battered women, who seldom complain and often hesitate to seek help, suffer from a variety of physical, emotional, and vague somatic symptoms: backaches, headaches, gastrointestinal symptoms, sleep disturbances, and nightmares, as well as anxiety and nervousness due to their husbands' unpredictable behavior. Their low self-esteem and low self-confidence leads them to become socially isolated, gradually drifting away from family and friends under the pretext of "being busy." Feeling powerless, frightened, and extremely dependent, many of them suppress their anger and hostility and find it hard to communicate and develop any relationship built on trust. Most victims become depressed and contemplate suicide due to their persistent feelings of hopelessness. Along with depression, victims of domestic violence may also experience PTSD, which is characterized by flashbacks, intrusive imagery, nightmares, anxiety, emotional numbing, insomnia, hyper-vigilance, avoidance of traumatic triggers, and similar symptoms. Several empirical studies have explored the relationship between experiencing domestic violence and developing PTSD (Vitanza S., Vogel, L.C. et. al, 1995). Even after separation and divorce, some of these symptoms continue for a long period of time. Domestic violence does not end until outside intervention has taken place.

The cycle of violence

The cycle of violence is described in three stages: the tension building stage (tension in the relationship gradually increases over time); the acute battering stage (tension erupts, resulting in threats or use of violence and abuse); and the honeymoon stage (the batterer may be apologetic and remorseful and promise not to be abusive again) (Hattendorf, J. and Tollerud, T.R., 1997). The husband hits the wife, and she considers it a one-time occurrence; he hits her again, and the behavior continues. She temporary moves to a family or a friend's house. He makes frequent calls, apologizes, and asks her to return. She returns home, and things are better for a few days. However, the pattern of abuse recurs. The threat and the mild abuse turn into a severe blow on the face. Fearing for her life, she leaves home and goes with her children to her sister's or friend's house. She is in a dilemma over whether or not to report her husband to the police. If she reports him, he will be put in jail and/or deported, resulting in shame, guilt, a loss of income, and possibly more reprisals. She worries about how she will support the children and is concerned about her limited resources. Many victims of domestic violence do not get support from family members and/or religious institutions.

The cycle continues throughout the relationship, with the honeymoon stage becoming shorter and the episodes of battering becoming more frequent or more severe. Many women go through this scenario and face serious difficulties when trying to decide whether to stay in the relationship or leave. Few years ago, I saw an attorney's wife who had to make this difficult decision and eventually gave up a comfortable life for an uncertain future of serious economic hardship to get away from the persistent physical abuse inflicted upon her by her husband of fifteen years. She had to spend several months in a shelter before settling down in the community and getting a modest paying job.

For many women, abusive relationships continue for years. Even after leaving the abusive husband, research indicates that the women return home six to seven times during the relationship. The critical issue appears to be the emotional break from the abuser, which only occurs after the victim consciously realizes the danger and risks of her situation. Many immigrant women stay in an abusive relationship for years due to the lack of available resources, language barriers, and limited skills. Many immigrant women feel that they have no option but to go on living with the abusive husband.

Arguments occur at some point among all spouses. Verbally abuse may occur during arguments about childcare, housework, and financial matters. Domestic violence is different from routine arguments and expressions of anger. Similarly, in certain cultures women are encouraged to stay at home and are not allowed to drive cars. Such examples of inequality and oppression should not be confused or equated with domestic violence, for in the latter case the abusers show a complex pattern of verbal and physically aggressive behavior designed to control the victim. Sometime religious and community leaders are unable to differentiate between common anger and abusive behavior, and thus victims are told to be patient, tolerant, and avoid conflict.

Domestic violence is a universal problem

All ethnic, religious, racial, and age groups are effected by domestic violence (Bachman, R. and Saltzman, L.E., 1995). African-American women experience domestic violence at a much higher rate than White and Hispanic women. In fact, the number one killer of African-American women aged

15-34 is homicide at the hand of their spouse or partner (Africana Voices Against Violence, 2002). Seventy-seven percent of Hispanic women residing in Texas indicate that they, a family member, or a friend have experienced some form of domestic violence, and 46% of them acknowledge that leaving the abusive relationship can be more dangerous than staying (Texas Council on Family Violence, Statistics, 2002). Among Asian women, 12.8% of them reported experiencing physical assault by their spouse at least once in their lifetime. The rate is lower than those reported by White (21.3%) and African-American (26.3%) women (Tjaden, P. and Thoennes, N., 2000). Asian women usually under report their abuse due to language and cultural barriers, as well as the lack of available services. Domestic violence is a serious problem among immigrants in the United States. One study in New York found that 51% of all intimate partner homicide victims were immigrants (New York City DOH, Femicide in New York City: 1995-2002, 2004).

Very few studies have measured the extent and nature of domestic violence within specific religious groups. Recently, some articles and books have appeared on domestic violence from the Jewish and Islamic perspectives. Jewish Women International indicates that 15 to 25 percent of Jewish women experience domestic violence, and statistics show that they remain in abusive relationships five to seven years longer than non-Jewish women (Abuse Does Not Discriminate, 2003). According to estimates by Muslim activists in the United States, approximately 10 percent of Muslim women are abused emotionally, psychologically, and/or physically by their husbands (Faizi, N., 2001).

The Southern Baptist's justification for domestic abuse

One reason that men abuse their wives, according to Bruce Ware, a professor of Christian theology at Southern Baptist Theological Seminary in Louisville, KY, is because women rebel against their husband's God-given authority. He also stated in a recent meeting at a church in Denton, TX that the "*fact*" that women desire to have their own way instead of submitting to their husbands because of sin. "And husbands on their parts, because they're sinners, now respond to that threat to their authority either by being abusive, which is of course one of the ways men can respond when their authority is challenged—or, more commonly, to become passive, acquiescent, and simply not asserting the leadership they ought to as men in their homes and in churches."

He offered several reasons "for affirming male headship in the created order." They include that man was created first and that woman was created "out of" Adam in order to be his "helper." Even though Eve sinned first, Ware said, God came to Adam and held him primarily responsible for failure to exercise his God-given authority. "Eve was tempted and deceived by the serpent and ate the forbidden fruit, and then gave it also to Adam," Ware stated. "Eve, that is, sinned first. Despite this fact, God seeks out Adam after their sin to inquire why they were hiding . . . God approaches Adam, not Eve, as the one ultimately responsible for the sin. Adam only rightly bears the responsibility as the head of the sinful human race, when Eve sinned first, if he is viewed by God . . . as having authority and ultimate responsibility over the woman," Ware posited (Allen, B., 2008).

Certainly these statements will give the abuser a rationale to justify his behavior and will deprive women of any support from religious leaders. And, unfortunately, they will remain in an abusive relationship for years.

Contrary to expected behavior, religious leaders are also involved in abusive behavior toward women. Last year, an African-American female television evangelist from Atlanta was severely choked and kicked by her husband, who is himself a minister. Another woman murdered her preacher husband, citing continuous psychological and physical abuse and harassment.

Abusive treatment of Muslim women

Muslim men commonly understand Qur'anic Verse 4:34 as giving them the sanction to exert power and control over women and abuse them, if necessary: "Men are the protectors and maintainers of women, because God has given the one more (strength) than the other, and because they support them from their means. Therefore the righteous women are devoutly obedient and guard in (the husband's) absence what God would have them guard. As to those women on whose part you fear disloyalty and ill-conduct, admonish them (first). (Next,) refuse to share their beds. (And last,) beat them (lightly). But if they return to obedience, seek not against them means (of annoyance), for God is Most High, Great (above you all)." (Qur'an (4:34))

This verse explains that men are charged with providing for their families in financial terms, as well as with protecting and taking care of them, because God has made men physically stronger; women, in turn, are expected to guard their husbands' property and their own fidelity. If women ignore God's command about sexual fidelity and become disloyal to their husbands, the penalties are clear. Unfortunately, some scholars misinterpret the verse and give husbands the authority to oversee the wife's behavior under all circumstances. It is not uncommon for husbands to prevent their wives from going outside the house, meeting relatives and friends, and seeking education and jobs. Some Muslim men actually use Islam to "justify" their abusive behavior. Considering themselves knowledgeable about Islam and disregarding its spirit, they wrongly use Qur'an 4:34 to go on power trips, demand total obedience, and disregard the Islamic requirement that the head of the household must consult with other members of the family when making decisions.

If the wife is accused of being disloyal to her husband, the verse outlines the necessary steps to be taken: "Admonish them (first). (Next,) refuse to share their beds. (And last,) beat them (lightly)." Even the meaning of "beat them (lightly)" is misinterpreted, for some scholars say that this also means the men separating or removing themselves from their wives. If their wives dare to speak up or question their orders, these men misinterpret a Qur'anic verse that talks about how to treat a disobedient wife and do not hesitate to abuse her.

Unfortunately, Muslim women often accept this un-Islamic treatment because they are ignorant of their rights under Islam and do not realize that their husbands have crossed the line. Abusive men completely disregard the Islamic teachings of kindness, mercy, gentleness, and forgiveness, just as they disregard the example of Prophet Muhammad (peace be upon him), who never hit a woman and was extremely gentle and compassionate to all of his family members.

Violence against women is a global phenomenon

Due to the lack of statistics, it is hard to know the extent of such abuse in developing countries. Recently, however, reports of abuse in Pakistan, India, Iran, Bangladesh, and Egypt have appeared. Previously, these cases were not reported. Globally 30% of women are beaten or sexually assaulted in their lifetime. Raping women is widespread all over the world, especially during war and army conflicts. In Saudi Arabia, a young woman who was gang raped by seven men was sentenced to six months imprisonment and 200 lashes for being alone with a man who was not from her immediate family. After worldwide media publicity, she was released. Similar incidents have occurred in Pakistan and other Muslim countries.

The perpetrators are morally and legally responsible for the abusive behavior. To ostracize or condemn the victim for engaging in sexual acts against her will is a violation of her human rights. Surprisingly, 102 members of the United Nations have no specific laws that criminalize domestic violence. Despite its commitment to protect women and girls from violence, the violence against them continues. The U.S. Senate is now considering the International Violence against Women Act (IVAWA), which Senators Joseph Biden and Richard Lugar introduced in October 2007. This comprehensive bill would use diplomatic influence to prevent many brutal forms of violence, such as honor killing (the Middle East), bride burning (India), female genital mutilation (Africa), mass rapes (in such war-torn nations as Bosnia, Rwanda, and Sudan [Darfur]), and support laws against abusive behavior toward women by intimate partners (the United States). Unfortunately, this law has not been passed during the last session of the congress (International Violence Against Women Act of 2007.) Although brutal forms of violence exist globally, it is especially sad to see that the high rates of violence and death caused by domestic violence in the world's most civilized country, namely, the United States.

Violence against women and girls is a global epidemic that affects the health and economic stability of women, their families, and their communities. These victims are often unable or afraid to seek health care, and the ongoing violence can prevent them from participating in their community's socioeconomic life. Women in developing nations face serious challenges. Research consistently shows that intimate partner violence against women has serious consequences for maternal mortality and child survival (World Development Report, 1993 and Heise, L. et. al, 1999).

Abused women run twice the risk of miscarriage and four times the risk of having a below-average-weight baby (World Development Report, 1993). The prevalence of women in developing countries who experience violence during pregnancy ranges from 4 to 20 percent (Nasir, K. and Hyder, A., 2003). In Nicaragua, research shows that children of women abused by their partners were six times more likely to die before the age of five than other children. A recent study in India showed that intimate partner violence caused 16% of maternal deaths during pregnancy (Heise, L. et. al, 1999). Another study found that 43.5% of women reported that they were psychologically abused by their partners, and 40.3% reported that they were physically abused. Fifty percent of physically abused women reported violence during pregnancy (International center for research on women, 2003). All pregnant women attending their first antenatal clinic in a Chinese community hospital were interviewed to detect the incidence of domestic violence as well as its nature, frequency, and perpetrator: 17.9% had a history of abuse, 15.7% had been abused in the last year, and 4.3% had been abused during their current pregnancy by their husbands (Leung, T. et. al, 1999)

In forty-eight population-based surveys from around the world, 10 to 69 percent of women reported being physically assaulted by an intimate male partner at some point in their lives (Krug, E. et. al 2002). Unfortunately, in developing countries like India, authorities seldom pay attention to family violence, with the result that women suffer for many years at the hands of their husbands. A recent BBC report showed that in eastern India, women have united and start taking actions against their husbands' persistent abuse and the lack of support from police and other officials. "In cases of domestic violence, we go and talk to the man and explain why it is wrong. If he refuses to listen, we get the woman out of the house and then beat him. If necessary, we do it in public to embarrass him. Men used to think the law didn't apply to them, but we are forcing a huge change" (Biswas, S., 2007).

The role of the community

The global community has clearly failed to protect women from abuse and to bring the perpetrators to justice. Several countries do not even have laws against domestic violence. The community needs to deal much more effectively with women's abuse in order to stop the immediate suffering of those living in an abusive situation and to help build healthy families. Unless community and religious leaders, and especially men, take the major responsibility to eradicate this problem, it will continue. Unfortunately, some community "leaders" do not have the knowledge or training to deal with these issues.

The current situation

In the United States, domestic violence remains a serious problem. For the immigrant community, however, domestic violence is a more serious threat due to cultural and language barriers and the lack of available resources. Many immigrants in such situations seek help at local shelters. Religious and cultural barriers, however, make them uncomfortable, and many women are hesitant to seek help. Many shelter staff members also feel uncomfortable and frustrated due to the lack of knowledge about the immigrants' religions and cultures. Therefore, it is very important that they become familiar with the uniqueness of their clients' different cultures and religions, especially of those coming from South Asia and the Middle East. Cross-cultural training programs are essential to alleviating this problem. In addition, they must recruit counselors and community workers from all immigrant communities.

Prevention Strategies

The primary goal of prevention is to reduce the incidence of a problem in a population before it occurs. Primary prevention strategies can introduce to community groups the new values, thinking processes, respect, trust, and relationship skills needed to promote a healthy and non-violent relationship (Wolfe, D. et. al, 1999 and Millstein, S.G., et. al, 1993). Secondary prevention measures target individuals in order to decrease the problem's prevalence by reducing its severity and its early manifestations. The focus here is on identifying the victims of abusive behavior and offering them assistance so that they can deal effectively with abusive situations. Tertiary prevention measures attempt to minimize the problem's course once it has been identified and started to cause harm. Here, the main goal is to identify domestic violence, as well as its perpetrators and victims, and then take legal action and institute treatment for the perpetrators and support for the victims. Making a commitment to undertake comprehensive efforts to stop domestic violence and prevent future acts requires very intensive work (Albee, G. 1985). One comprehensive public education campaign developed by the Family Violence Prevention Fund (FVPF) included television advertisements stating that there is no excuse for domestic violence and providing information about local domestic violence services (Klein, E., et. al, 1997).

Community Education Program

Community and religious leaders need to be educated about the problem and the efforts to help victims. They can gain this knowledge by attending educational seminars and workshops that will inform them in no uncertain terms that that the community at large will no longer tolerate such behavior. Such an approach will reduce incidents of abuse. Furthermore, the community needs to establish classes to teach young men how to be proper husbands and fathers, and to teach young women how to be proper wives and mothers. Many women do not know their rights and obligations in these roles. In addition, in order to prevent future family problems, parents and community leaders must teach children and young adults to be compassionate, value the family, and resolve problems in a non-violent manner.

Domestic Violence and Role of Religious Leaders

Religious leaders vary in their familiarity with the issues facing victims of domestic violence. Some leaders are very interested in social issues, attend seminars, and become knowledgeable about the psychodynamics of abuse. Others continue to live in denial, saying that they do not come across such problems and that they do not exist. Some even justify abusive behavior saying that women's behavior must be corrected by punitive means as needed.

There is an element in religious belief, especially in scriptures, of male dominance. Most of the time, however, such interpretations are taken out of context to serve the purpose of the male-dominant society. No religion sanctions violence against women. On many occasions, women's lack of confidence and low self-esteem allows them to tolerate such abuse. Religious leaders must be aware of this problem, show compassion, and be willing to work with abused women as well as with the abusers. Domestic violence and abusive behavior, which may be a learned phenomenon, can be unlearned. The abuser, who may not be an evil person, should be guided to receive appropriate treatment if he is interested in having a harmonious relationship. The perpetrator must understand and recognize that his behavior is hurtful and harmful, accept responsibility for his behavior, and understand that a woman does not have to stay in a violent home.

In the case of Muslim women who are abused, the community's religious leaders and the mosque may play a vital role in providing appropriate support, rehabilitation, and spiritual comfort. Most Muslim immigrants come from male-dominant societies in which women stay at home and seldom play a major role in decision making. Religious leaders can play a significant role by providing their community members with a clear understanding on this subject, especially during Friday sermons and especially organized community meetings. A close relationship between religious leaders and social service organizations will help alleviate this problem in the Muslim community. We all must work together to stop violence against women.

The Father's Role

A father can play a significant role in teaching his sons how to express their anger without using violence, such as talking it out, taking a time out, or going for a walk. Fathers must make an effort to watch television or read news items related to domestic violence with their sons and then discuss situations depicting violence against women. All jokes, video games, lyrics, and sports figures that demean women should be condemned. Boys are heavily influenced by the external environment (namely, television, the Internet, music, movies, and their friends), and therefore must be taught to treat girls and women with respect. Fathers need to be aware of how they express their own anger, especially when dealing with people while driving in traffic, talking with customer service representatives or waitresses, and with other individuals they meet during the day. Thousands of men across the country are taking a stand against domestic violence by joining such organizations as the Founding Fathers (www.founding-fathers.org).

Conclusion

Women and men are equal and must be treated with equal dignity and respect. Therefore, it is necessary that all forms of violence against women be eradicated. As long as women are abused, humiliated, and degraded, they cannot achieve their full human potential as free and equal members of our society. Holding perpetrators accountable is a significant first step toward eliminating such violence. Health care providers, physicians, nurses, councilors, and religious leaders must familiarize themselves with the cross-cultural perspectives of domestic violence and understand the unique challenges they face in handling such situations. In addition, community and religious leaders must realize that a significant number of cases go unreported and that those women need help. These leaders must play a significant role in alleviating this problem within the community and help devise regulations that prohibit any kind of violence against women.

We have tolerated this evil behavior for a long time, and now it is time that we need to pay serious attention to eliminating it from our society. Religious and community leaders, health and human service professionals, legal professionals, and legislative members must work together to achieve a common goal: stop the violence against women.

References

Abuse Does Not Discriminate, July 2003 http://www.hadassah.org/

Africana Voices Against Violence, Tufts University, Statistics, 2002, www.ase.tufts.edu/womenscenter/peace/africana/newsite/statistics.htm

Albee, G. "The Argument for Primary Prevention" Journal of Primary Prevention 5:213-19 1985

Allen, B., "Southern Baptist Scholar Links Spouse Abuse to Wives' Refusal to Submit to Their Husband", from Ethicsdaily.com, Posted: Friday, June 27, 2008.

Bachman R., Saltzman L.E., "Violence against women: estimates from the redesigned survey. A National crime victim action report" Bureau of Justice statistics. U.S. Department of Justice, NCJ 154:348, 1995

Biswas, S., *"India's 'pink' vigilante woman"*, BBC, 2007, *http://news.bbc.co.uk/go/pr/fr/-/2/hi/south_asia/7068875.stm*

Children Now/Kaiser Permanente poll," (December 1995).

Danielson K.K. et al., "Comorbidity Between Abuse of an Adult and DSM-III-R Mental Disorders: Evidence From an Epidemiological Study," American Journal of Psychiatry 1998; 155:131-133

Duhart D.T., U.S. Department of Justice, NCJ 190076, Violence in the Workplace 1993-99, Bureau of Justice Statistics Special Report (2001). Available at *www.ojp.usdoj.gov/bjs/pub/pdf/vw99.pdf.*

Dutton, D.G., & Painter, S.L. (1981). Traumatic bonding: The development of emotional attachments in battered women and other relationships of intermittent abuse. *"Victimology: An International Journal", 1,* 139-155.

Faizi, N. (2001). Domestic Violence in Muslim communities. Texas Journal of Women and the Law, 10, 209-230.

Flit Craft A.H., Hadley S.M., Hendricks, Mathews M.K. et al., *Diagnostic & Treatment Guidelines on Domestic Violence* (Chicago: American Medical Association, 1992), 244.

Graham-Bermann, S. and Seng, J., "Violence Exposure and Traumatic Stress Symptoms as Additional Predictors of Health Problems in High-Risk Children" *Journal of Pediatrics.* Volume 146, Issue 3, March 2005, Pages 349-354

Greenfeld L.A., Rand M.R. et al, U.S. Deptartment of Justice, "Violence by Intimates: Analysis of Data on Crimes by Current or Former Spouses, Boyfriends and Girlfriends," March 1998.

Harway, M. & Hansen, M. (1994). *Spouse abuse: Assessing and treating battered women, batterers, and their children.* Sarasota, Florida: Professional Resource Press.

Hattendorf, J. & Tollerud, T.R. (1997). Domestic violence: Counseling strategies that minimize the impact of secondary victimization. *Perspectives in Psychiatric Care, 33,* 14-23.

Heise, L., Ellsberg, M. and Gottemoeller, M., 1999. "Ending Violence Against Women." *Population Reports.* Series L, No.11. Johns Hopkins University School of Public Health, Population Information Program. Baltimore, Maryland.

International center for research on women, *"Domestic Violence in India: A summary report of multi-site household survey",* Washington D.C., 2003.

International Violence Against Women Act of 2007, *http://www.govtrack. us/congress/bill.xpd?bill=s110-2279*

Jaffe, P. and Suderman, M., "Child Witness of Woman Abuse: Research and Community Response," in Smiths C. and Strauss M., U*nderstanding Partner Violence Prevalence, Causes, Consequences, and Solutions: Families in Focus Services* Vol. II (Minneapolis: National Council on Family relations, 1995).

Klein, E., Campbell, J., Soler, E., et al., *"Ending Domestic Violence",* Sage Publications, Thousand Oaks, CA, 1997.

Krug, E., Dalhberg, L., Mercy, J., et al. *"World Report on Violence and Health",* World Health Organization, Geneva, Switzerland, 2002. http:// www.who.int/violence_injury_prevention/violence/world_report/en/ FullWRVH.pdf

Leung, T. Leung, Y. Lam, P "The prevalence of domestic violence against pregnant women in a Chinese community. Social issues in reproductive health. International Journal of Gynecology & Obstetrics, Volume 66, Issue 1, Pages 23-30, July 1999.

McFarlane, Judith, et al., "Assessing for Abuse During Pregnancy," *Journal of the American Medical Association*, June 17, 1992.

Domestic Violence: A Cross-Cultural Perspective

The Power of One

Najma M. Adam, Ph.D.

SOME OF THE complexity regarding cross-cultural domestic violence can really be simplified to at least one fundamental fact that we all know too well: domestic violence happens in all cultures, and therefore in all religions and societies, despite some people's defensive stance that their culture/religion/group is somehow immune to this intractable social problem.

Generally, culture includes life patterns passed on from generation to generation and includes institutions, values, beliefs, language, customs, religion, thinking, artistic expressions, and patterns of social and interpersonal relationships. Given this definition, it is evident that we are all a part of at least one culture, if not multiple cultural groups. Many of us can navigate through cultures and subcultures with ease. Culture, which provides us with a sense of belonging, acceptance, and comfort, makes and shapes us. It is inherently how we become who we are currently, and new cultural influences change and keep us reinventing parts of ourselves . . . or at least they should.

Culture is relevant to domestic violence because it is one of the culprits that create the conditions that initiate, foster, and maintain domestic violence against women, children, the elderly, and yes, even men. So we have two rather clear facts before us: domestic violence cuts across all cultural groups (including religious and socioeconomic), and some cultural patterns within all cultural groups initiate and support domestic violence. But you know this already, and I have not come here to share the obvious with you. To discuss cultural competency across different cultural groups, particularly as it relates to domestic violence, would result in a rather lengthy list of dos and don'ts, and that is not how I want to spend our limited time together.

Rather, I would like to talk about solutions, an issue that I believe must be forced into greater prominence in the domestic violence field so that we can move beyond the obvious and into action. In this way, perhaps the suffering of many individuals can be impacted positively. So, the question I would like to explore with you is how we can change those aspects of culture that are responsible for domestic violence. Together, we should be able to tackle this question in the next half hour. As I think about this, I come up with multiple cultural levels that must be targeted. Moreover, in my thinking, it is important to think of solutions that each one of us can do immediately, perhaps so that the theoretical construction of solutions can be easily accessed and realized. Now, I am no fool either. I realize that solutions take time and that transforming deeply held sociocultural and religious beliefs may appear next to impossible to alter. Yet, I find much inspiration in the "starfish story." You remember the little girl who picked up one starfish at a time and threw it back into the water. An adult said to her that her actions did not matter, because too many starfish were dying. And her response was that it would matter to the one being hurled back into the water. I firmly believe that if each one of us had that little girl's perspective, we could collectively impact and create a change, however slight, that would yield positive results for the many people who suffer needlessly . . . a simple idea really, and not mine, but that of many good souls who believe in the power of one.

For example, let's begin with the micro-perspective and think about parenting. Would it not be ideal if parents everywhere, regardless of ethnicity, religion, or socioeconomic class would allow their children to adopt gender roles that are flexible rather than rigid and prescribed? In this way, perhaps boys can learn that it is okay to wash dishes and cry, and girls can learn that they can play with cars or fix them if they choose to do so, without being ostracized. If gender roles are not strictly adhered to, as they largely tend to be in our society, perhaps as adults these individuals may relate to one another as equal human beings with different interests and strengths, and not according to the obligatory roles that must be fulfilled to satisfy tradition. How does this relate to domestic violence? Ultimately, you see, these rigid roles, which create the machismo man or the subservient woman, are linked to domestic violence. In part, these roles create a system based on which gender is superior and which one is inferior, whose work is valued and whose is not, and which gender is to be treated as an object and which one is to be relished.

Have you ever considered what kind of change we could force if one of us would complain whenever the media aired, in whatever medium, demeaning, dehumanizing, and objectifying pictures of women (or in some instances men)? Perhaps then girls and women would not starve themselves to death to achieve a superficial notion of beauty; instead, they could concentrate on the beauty that comes from building oneself from within. What if women and men boycotted those hedonistic beauty pageants, or if women themselves simply stopped participating in such events because they have more pride in their character then in their external features? Have you ever met people who appeared unattractive to you at first and then, when you got to know them, their habits, personality, character, sense of integrity, confidence, and self-respect, you suddenly changed your mind about their attractiveness? This is evidence that beauty comes from within.

How does this connect to domestic violence? When the media projects images that dehumanize women (largely), this message is successfully inculcated in men and women, boys and girls. Thus, in intimate relationships women and girls are beaten, kicked, stabbed, slapped, or murdered because, well, she is just another object, right? Not another human being with feelings, desires, dreams, and hopes. Just think about the potential of this change, which would mean that boys and men would no longer be given a message that largely sees women as simply objects to do with as they please and then discard when they are finished. Women would no longer have to feel that their lives are less valuable, less privileged, or less worthy than a man's. What if each one of us committed to voting, regardless of the level, for candidates who work to remedy violence rather than create it, whether it takes place in families, schools, communities, or nationally or even internationally? This would mean reducing the availability of guns and taking measures that begin to create a safer society for all of us. What if each one of us held our politicians accountable, rather than allowing them a cushy position with many benefits and little accountability? It seems to me that somewhere along the way in our "democratic" system, politicians forgot that they work for us, not the other way around. In social work, I have heard it said that it only takes three individuals to complain about an issue before a representative will take action—just three. Look around. How many of us are in this room? What if each one of us demanded appropriate political, diplomatic, and legal remedies to violence? This is not just a theoretical discourse. Remember "Tank Man," the man known as "Unknown Rebel," who, during the Tiananmen Square protests in June 1989, stood in front of a procession of Chinese tanks to prevent their advance? This is the power of one, and each one of us can contribute so that domestic violence against others may end.

Religious culture in all religions must be changed so that compassion, service, love, and kindness may prevail. Each one of us holds the power to demand that those who lead our churches, temples, synagogues, mandirs, and mosques preach a message consistent with the core values of all religions. What if we stopped attending our respective places of worship unless the message of peace was the only one to be preached? Imagine the effect of such an action. What if each one of us stopped contributing financially to such places unless they preach and practice the equality of both sexes? I, for one, am tired of imams who only preach the same tired, outdated, and self-serving message of how God wants us all to "obey and respect" our husbands (i.e., men). The God of Justice and Fairness, it would seem to me, would advocate mutual obedience and respect. After all, what kind of God would create women to be 51 percent of the population and then send down a message that men should treat them as inferior beings; to hate, slap, kick, beat, hurt, and destroy them both from within as well as through such acts as burning, slicing, cutting, and murdering? My intellect tells me that patriarchy, not God, demands that women know their "rightful place." The insiders of these groups must criticize ethno-cultural practices that excuse domestic violence. I, for one, am tired of hearing about how "this is our way" or "this is how it is in our culture." Domestic violence is still domestic violence, no matter how some individuals attempt to shroud it in "culture." A perpetrator is a perpetrator and a victim is a victim, no matter what other identities they hold. Courageous insiders who criticize their negative cultural practices ought to be supported by insiders and outsiders. Instead, too often, they are criticized by other insiders as being "undiplomatic," "too abrasive," "inappropriate," and on and on. In other words, "we do not want to change." Just think of the power of one individual standing with another who speaks out against domestic violence anchored in negative cultural practices. And if each one of us stands together in our ethnic cultural groupings, we can—and must—demand change.

Cultural practices are not static, and those that destroy, hurt, or wreak havoc on others must be changed. Loyalties must not be to one's cultural practices, cultural group, or social or economic status, but to the greater ideal of social justice, which demands that all human beings have a right to a life free of violence, that they are valuable individuals with integrity and worth. I realize that it is challenging to critique cultural practices as an insider, let alone as an outsider. But yet I ask those of you who stand for social justice and human rights to partner with the insiders and take a stand against violence within those communities where ethno-cultural practices harm, destroy, and sometimes end the valuable lives of others. Great changes have taken place when human beings have come together for a common cause. Consider what happened when White Americans stood with Black Americans during the Civil Rights movement. Unfortunately, our hyper-sensitivity to cultures and their practices has also yielded an environment in which criticism of inhumane cultural practices, like those that support domestic violence against anyone, is beyond reproach.

I leave you with this one final thought and urge you to consider taking action: keep in mind that the power of one—you—can make a difference. I ask you to begin examining domestic violence through a cross-cultural perspective by examining your own beliefs, values, and attitudes. If you have not taken action in any of the areas mentioned already, why not? If you have, then your final charge is to urge others around you to take action. Convince them of the power of one. Let's move ahead in the belief that, fundamentally, each one of us has an inherent right to respect, dignity, and a life free of violence. Let's work toward this goal now.

*   The author is indebted to her department chair, Dr. Gerri Outlaw, and her colleagues, Drs. Maristela Zell, Betsy Essex, and Kim Boland-Prom for their support.

Family Relations: An Islamic Perspective

Zainab Alwani, Ph.D.

ISLAM, AS GOD'S final message to humanity, came to light in a brutal and cruel environment. Violence was a common practice in pre-Islamic Arabia, and the weak and the needy, orphans and widows, and slaves and servants, both there and around the world, had no defined rights. Islam came to establish justice and mercy in the heart of a cruel world. The Qur'an emphasizes that all people are created equal as regards their inherent worth and value, regardless of race, ethnicity, gender, or class. Islam prohibited any oppressive behavior that violates justice, mercy, equality, and freedom.

In light of this, the Qur'an revolutionized the status of women by critically analyzing and reforming various local and global customs and traditions related to gender relations. Women were not even considered human beings in pre-Islamic Arabia; Islam recognized them as full human beings and as equal to men before God:

"O humanity, reverence your Lord, who created you from a single soul, and created, of like nature, its mate, and from them twain scattered (like seeds) countless men and women. Reverence God, through whom you demand your mutual (rights), and (reverence) the wombs (that bore you), for God ever watches over you." (4:1). One of the most grotesque abuses against women at the time was female infanticide. Men who were ashamed of their daughters buried them alive (Qur'an 16:58 and 81:8-9). The Qur'an abolished this horrific act of violence by addressing it at various points. In addition, as women were considered the man's property, a man's brother or adult son could "inherit" the deceased man's wife and take her for himself without her consent (Qur'an 4:19). Qur'an 9:71 established that men and women were considered partners of each other, for in this verse God makes it clear that both of them have the same obligation to enjoin what is good and forbid what is evil. In other words, men have no level of moral authority over women, and both men and women are obliged to keep each other on the straight path and prevent each other from going astray:

The believers, men and women, are protectors one of another (*awliya*). They enjoin what is good and forbid what is evil. They observe regular prayers, practice regular charity, and obey God and His Messenger. On them will God pour His Mercy, for Allah is Exalted in Power, Wise. (9:71)

The Qur'an not only deconstructed unjust and misogynistic practices, but also offered practical and healthy alternatives. Consequently, most of the first Muslims were poor, slaves, and women. A justly balanced community soon evolved, enjoining what is good and forbidding what is evil.

In pre-Islamic Arabia, it was socially acceptable for a man to kill his wife if he suspected her of having an affair (Badawi, J., 1995). The Qur'an prohibited this grotesque act of violence and introduced reforms to protect the wife and women accused of immoral conduct by introducing less destructive ways to address the problem. For example, chapter 24 establishes the legal procedures for prosecuting adultery. A man's testimony against his wife is equivalent to her testimony in defense of herself. Even if she is lying, her testimony claiming innocence is enough to avert her punishment (Qur'an 24:8: "But it would avert the punishment from the wife, if she bears witness four times (with an oath of) by Allah, that (her husband) is telling a lie"). Furthermore, the same chapter prescribes a severe punishment for men who accuse chaste women of adultery without bringing sufficient evidence (four witnesses of upright character who witnessed the act of sexual intercourse firsthand). By establishing procedural principles for prosecuting adultery and other charges often raised against women, the Qur'an sent the message that husbands had no right to take the law into their own hands. If male witnesses could not produce sufficient evidence, or if a wife denied the charges made by her husband, no punishment was enacted.

The Controversy Surrounding Quranic Verse 4:34

In this context, the Qur'an also addressed a wife's lewd conduct (*nushuz*) in verse 4:34 (Qur'an 4:34-35: "And as for those women whose (*nushuz*) lewd conduct, you have reason to fear, admonish them [first]; then leave them alone in bed; then hit them (lightly) [*daraba*]. And if thereupon they pay you heed, do not seek to harm them. Behold, God is indeed Most High, Great. And if you have reason to fear that a breach might occur between a [married] couple, appoint an arbiter from among his people and an arbiter from among her people. If they both want to set things aright, God may bring about their reconciliation. Behold, God is indeed All-Knowing, Aware.").

While this verse has been the subject of great controversy due to the term *daraba*, which is mistranslated as "to beat," this verse in no way sanctions domestic violence. First, the primary means of Qur'anic interpretation applied by scholars is to read the Qur'an intra-textually, known as *tafsir al-Qur'an bil Qur'an* (allowing the Qur'an to interpret itself). Hence, it is critical to understand verse 4:34 in light of the Qur'an's overall gender paradigm. Upon examining the countless verses governing marital relations, it becomes quite clear that the Qur'an demands that both partners treat each other with respect, justice, and mercy.

The second most important source that exegetes use to interpret the Qur'an is the Prophet (peace be upon him [pbuh]), whose life, words, and actions are regarded as a living commentary on the Qur'an and provide the framework within which *tafsir* is to be exercised. This mode is known as *tafsir bil-ma'thur* (interpretations transmitted through prophetic traditions [*hadith*]). When 4:34 is measured against the Prophet's (pbuh) constant condemnation of domestic violence in both word and deed, it becomes clear that this verse does not allow domestic violence, but rather condemns it.

In a number of authentic *ahadith* (Prophetic traditions), the Prophet (pbuh) prohibited domestic violence. For example, he said: "Never beat God's handmaidens (female believers)" (Asad, M., 1980). In reference to men who use violence at home, he asked: "Could any of you beat his wife as he would beat a slave and then lie with her in the evening?" (Sahih Bukhari, Vol. 7, book 62, no. 132). The Prophet (pbuh) was known to never hit a woman or a child. His wife Aisha (may Allah be pleased with her) is reported to have said: "The Prophet never beat any of his wives or servants. In fact, he did not strike anything with his hand, except if he were struggling in the cause of God." (*Fath al-Bari*, vol. 9, p. 249). He was a man whom Aisha described as having internalized the teachings of the Qur'an in his character and personality.

If the Prophet (pbuh) had internalized the Qur'an's teachings (His wife Aisha described the Prophet as a walking Qur'an) and never hit a woman or a child, then how could the Qur'an sanction domestic violence? The Prophet (pbuh) was put in several situations where he could have beaten his wives, had he chosen to understand verse 4:34 as allowing this. When he was faced with serious marital disputes, however, he never resorted to violence. Rather, he gave his wives the option of leaving or remaining with him: "O Prophet, say to your wives: 'If you desire the life of this world and its glitter, then come,

I will provide for your enjoyment and set you free in a handsome manner. But if you seek God and His Messenger and the Hereafter, verily God has prepared for the well-doers among you a great reward'" (33:28-29). This is why the contemporary researcher AbdulHamid AbuSulayman notes that the most accurate meaning of *daraba* is "to separate." After carefully analyzing all seventeen instances in which the Qur'an uses *daraba*, he concludes that the general connotations of its root form in the Qur'an means "to separate, to distance, to depart, to abandon, and so forth." (AbuSulayman AbdulHamid, A., 2003). After analyzing verse 4:34 within the Qur'an's overall framework, he concludes that *daraba* means the husband's temporary separation from his wife (AbuSulayman AbdulHamid, A., 2003).

This understanding is supported by the Prophet's (pbuh) actions, as explained above. Even when some people accused Aisha of adultery, he neither raised his hand nor even his voice against her (Even an assertion of adultery, a serious offense in the Islamic context, is grounds for a legal proceeding.). Instead, he allowed her to stay at her father's house for a month at her request, until the Qur'an established her innocence (Qur'an 24:11-20). As explained earlier, when the Prophet's (pbuh) wives complained against him, he gave them the option of leaving or remaining with him.

In a historical context in which a man did not need permission to beat his wife, the Qur'an restricted domestic violence by prescribing certain procedures to resolve a marital dispute in which a husband feared his wife's lewd conduct. First, it is important to note that 4:34 can be used only in a very specific situation: the wife is thought to be guilty of lewd conduct. Second, the Qur'an established certain procedures to which a husband must adhere when confronted with such a situation. First, he is to advise her. If she refuses to heed his verbal counsel or admonition, then he can respond by not sleeping with her, thereby giving her the chance to realize the risks involved if she does not resume her commitment to the marriage. Third, and finally, *daraba* suggests that the husband can tap her symbolically with something very light, like a tissue, which is the most traditional interpretation.

But even when this traditional interpretation is applied, in no way does it allow abusive behavior, as it clearly specifies that *daraba* is to operate symbolically in this context. Traditional scholars placed so many conditions upon this light "hitting" or "tapping" that they rendered it merely symbolic. Among these conditions is that a husband could only use a *siwak* (wooden toothbrush) or a folded handkerchief, and that he must not hit her or leave any marks. In this regard, 4:34 restricts the use of violence and can in no way be considered a license. As Jamal Badawi points out, this verse limits the severity of intervention, thereby preventing people from the excessive abuse that may occur if the steps had not been specified and limited to what they are (Badawi, J. 1995).

Regardless of the interpretation applied this verse in no way sanctions domestic violence. Therefore, such contemporary jurists as Dr. Taha Jabir Al-Alwani (President of the Graduate School of Islamic Social Sciences, Leesburg, Virginia, 2003) suggest that in today's societies, the third step (i.e., "hitting" the wife) might not be applicable. He bases his opinion on the legislative rulings of the Prophet's (pbuh) Companions and other jurists in this matter and in other areas of Islamic law where rulings take into consideration the given issues' specific circumstances and elements. Al-Alwani explains that jurists consider the purposes of marriage when deriving rulings from verses: fulfilling the conditions needed to live in tranquility and harmony, build family relationships and networks, and procreation. Any application of the Qur'an's teachings cannot contradict or undermine these goals. Sometimes, jurists apply a verse's literal meaning if doing so will achieve these goals; at other times, they apply a verse's spirit if the literal meaning hinders the achievement of these goals.

In the case of 4:34, emphasis is placed on the verse's spirit, which involves protecting the family unit from a real threat to its survival. In today's world, beating one's wife would surely lead to the very destruction of the family unit that this verse seeks to preserve. According to Al-Alwani's methodology, the last step of the three-step process in verse 4:34 might be no longer applicable, considering the changes in context and circumstances.

The Modern Context

Cruelty comes into view again in today's world in different forms. However, the cruelest violence is when it happens within the family. Such violence occurs every six to twenty seconds in the United States, the United Kingdom, and many other countries, including Islamic ones. Domestic violence, recognized as one of the complex global societal dilemmas, is defined as a "pattern of abusive behaviors used by someone to establish power and control over another person in a relationship. After a period of abuse, batterers are often apologetic, but as the cycle repeats the abuse usually gets worse over time" (*www.peacefulfamilies.org/aboutdv.html*). Experts agree that while the causes of these behaviors vary, the resulting violence is always the result of a complex interplay of psychological and social factors that have created an imbalance of power between the sexes, races, status, and other differences. Where there is an imbalance of power, power may be abused. And it is this, coupled with society's tolerance, which allows domestic violence to flourish (Horley, S., 2001).

The Islamic Paradigm

The Qur'an represents a comprehensive model to protect the family from any type of oppression. The essence of the Islamic paradigm is grounded in the concept of *tawhid* (God's Oneness and Uniqueness). Muslims believe that God created men and women to worship and serve Him as *khalifahs* (representatives or vicegerents of God): "Behold. Your Lord said to the angels: "I will create a vicegerent (trustee) on Earth" (2:30). The only aspect by which one person is deemed better than another in God's sight is that of piety: "O humanity, We created you from a single (pair) of a male and a female and made you into nations and tribes that you may know each other (not that you may despise each other). Verily, the most honored of you in God's sight is the most righteous of you . . ." (49:13).

Qur'anic teachings clearly outline the gender roles and relations through major concepts, such as (1) *Zawjiyah* (pairing), which establishes equality and cooperation: "O humanity, reverence your Lord, who created you from a single soul, and created, of like nature, its mate, and from them twain scattered (like seeds) countless men and women. Reverence God, through whom you demand your mutual (rights), and (reverence) the wombs (that bore you), for God ever watches over you" (4:1); (2) *Wilayah* (protectors of each other). The Qur'an outlines the relationship between men and women as partners (*awliya*) of one another in establishing a healthy family and just society. This concept, which was explained in Surat al-Tawbah and applied by Prophet Muhammad (pbuh), establishes that men have no superiority over women, as God orders both genders to guide and keep each other in check: "The believers, men and women, are protectors one of another (*awliya*). They enjoin what is good and forbid what is evil. They observe regular prayers, practice regular charity, and obey God and His Messenger. On them will God pour His Mercy, for Allah is Exalted in Power, Wise" (9:71); and (3) *Qiwamah*, the Qur'anic mandate that men are financially responsible for the family (Qur'an 4:34). As a result, women are free to take care of the family by being nurturers without having the added stress of earning an income. While men are obliged to work to support the family, women may or may not choose to work outside the home, depending on the family's circumstances. Accordingly, each gender has special qualities that better enable it to perform a certain societal role. When that role is fulfilled, then society as a whole functions more effectively (Abugideiri, S. and Alwani, Z., 2003).

As Qur'an 4:1 shows, Islam teaches that all people are created equal as regards their inherent worth and value, regardless of race or ethnicity, gender or class. It is important to make a distinction here between *identical* and *equal*. Islam recognizes that men and women have different abilities and strengths that complement each other. Although they differ physically and emotionally, their differences do not cause one gender to be superior to the other. While men and women are considered equal in God's sight, they have different roles to play as regards their attempts to live according to God's will. However, no higher value is placed on one role versus the other, since both men and women must work as partners to have healthy families and societies (Abugideiri, S. and Alwani, Z., 2003).

In order to implement this, the Qur'an addresses the following issues in great detail: family structure, gender roles, inheritance, and the rules of *mahram* (an unmarriageable kin with whom sexual intercourse would be considered incestuous,) marriage and divorce laws, reconciliation, and financial matters. The Qur'an and Sunnah emphasize the connection between justice and piety, accountability to God, and the significance of taking preventive measures to avoid injustice and oppression.

The Qur'an recognizes that historically, in many societies, men have had power over women. In pre-Islamic Arab society, for example, many women had very little or no property, status, and/or rights. Therefore, the Qur'an and the traditions of the Prophet warned men (husbands, fathers, brothers, or guardians) not to hurt or take advantage of them in any way. In times of conflict or discord, the reminder to be God-conscious when making choices and decisions was repeated over and over (Qur'an 65:1-12). These reminders emphasize the hierarchal relationship between each individual and God, which helps guide every other human relationship (Abugideiri, S. and Alwani, Z., 2003).

Unfortunately, many Muslim-majority societies have cultural values that conflict with this understanding of equality. In some cultures women have an inferior position, as evidenced by their limited legal rights or limited involvement in society. On the other hand, Westerners may view the position of women in other countries as inferior simply because it differs from the position of women in their own societies. For example, Muslim women may choose not to work outside the home because they do not need to do so and because it is the husband's moral and social obligation to support them. By not working, they may be taking advantage of their right to be supported and dedicate themselves more fully to taking care of their children or making some other contribution to society through their social activities. In this case, it may actually be a position of honor and respect not to work outside the home, acknowledging that being a mother and homemaker are real jobs in and of themselves.

The Islamic Perspective on Marriage

Marriage in Islam is noble and universally necessary, because it brings tranquility, progeny, and continuation of life with purity and responsibility. Marriage is an act of worship that provides a legitimate sexual relationship between a man and a woman and, most importantly, provides a vehicle for fulfilling humanity's divine purpose as God's vicegerents through procreation and human relations (Al Faruqi, I., 1992). Its foundation and purpose are as follows: "And among His signs is this: that He created for you mates from among yourselves, that you may dwell in tranquility with them, and He has put love and mercy between your (hearts). Verily in that are signs for those who reflect" (30:21). This verse can be taken as a reminder that both spouses are inherently equal and that the union between them is a peaceful and compassionate one.

As I wrote in my chapter "The Qur'anic Model for Harmony in Family Relations, God said: "They are your *libas* (garments) and you are their garments" (2:187). Garments protect us from the dirt and grime of the outside world, are the closest things to our bodies, and wrap us in comfort. Being naturally conscious of appearance, people take time to choose the style and color, as well as the time to clean, iron, and generally maintain their garments. When the various meanings of *libas* are translated into the context of a relationship, the parallels are obvious: Men and women are mutual garments for each other. They cover each other's weaknesses, serve as protection and comfort from the harsh elements of reality, and safeguard the precious intimacy and secrets shared between them (Alwani, Z., 2007).

When two individuals decide to unite in marriage, they are bound by a "solemn covenant." (Qur'an 4:21). Each person entering a marriage makes a covenant with God to adhere to the Qur'an and the Sunnah in fulfilling the obligations of the marital relationship. God is a witness over this marriage contract. Any behavior or interaction done with the intent of upholding the divine instruction will be rewarded by God in the Hereafter and, at the same time, will contribute to a healthy family unit. Likewise, God will punish all behaviors that violate the divine instruction, including the foundation of mercy and love.

It is important to remember that the Muslim family structure is part of a larger context within the overall Islamic paradigm of holding men responsible for maintaining the family financially (Qur'an 4:34). Men are responsible for providing a broad range of spiritual, emotional, educational, and other needs. Without this divine law, some of them may not fulfill their financial responsibility toward their family and women are then freed to take care of the family by providing nurture and care, without having the added stress of earning an income.

Men and women are partners in maintaining a healthy family unit in which children are raised to be God-conscious members of society. The Qur'an sets up the framework for different roles that are equal in value and complementary. Each gender has special qualities that, in general, lead it to be better qualified for a particular role. The Qur'an says: "And do not covet that by which God has made some of you excel others. Men shall have the benefit of what they earn, and women shall have the benefit of what they earn. And ask God of His grace. Surely God knows all things" (4:32).

The fact that husband and wife have different roles in no way suggests that men are better than, or have God-given power over, women. Furthermore, these roles are not mutually exclusive, for both parents must be involved in raising the children. Although each may participate in different aspects of the child's upbringing, both are equally responsible for the child's overall welfare. *Shura* (mutual consultation), an important practical principle and tool rooted in the Islamic teaching, is designed to be used as an essentially a decision-making process among equals, for the envisaged goal is the reaching of a collective decision (Qur'an 2:233 and 42:38).

The fact that women are the primary managers of household affairs does not mean that husbands should not help or that women are restricted exclusively to this role. Prophet Muhammad (PBUH), the model husband, used to help with such domestic chores as sweeping and mending his clothes (Abu Shaqqah, 1990) and Aisha became a noted leader and teacher to many men who consulted her after her husband's death.

Distortions of Religious Teachings

Islam frequently and decisively prohibits any form of oppression, which can be defined as "an unjust or cruel exercise of authority or power" (*Webster's Ninth New Collegiate Dictionary*, 1983). The philosophy or objective of this ruling is designed to resolve problems that occur in human society and to present an alternative model.

These statements may contradict what is said by people who do not have an adequate understanding of the Islamic paradigm. Sometimes, Muslims themselves may take verses or sayings of the Prophet (pbuh) out of context to justify their behavior. Such manipulation of religious teachings should be viewed as the same type of behavior that abusers of other faiths engage in to justify their actions. One example of this is the practice of polygamy. As Karen Armstrong writes in her book *Muhammad: A Prophet for Our Time*

The Qur'anic institution of polygamy was a piece of social legislation. It was designed not to gratify the male sexual appetite, but to correct the injustice done to widow, orphans, and other female dependants, who were especially vulnerable. They were often sexually abused by their male guardians or converted into a financial asset by being sold into slavery. Polygamy was designed to ensure that unprotected women would be decently married, and to abolish the old loose, irresponsible liaisons; men could have only four wives and must treat them equitably, it was an unjustifiably wicked act to devour their property. The Qur'an was attempting to give women a legal status that most Western women would not enjoy until the nineteenth century" (Armstrong, K., 2006).

Another example of the abuse of religious law occurs in the case of marital discord or a serious dispute within the family. The Qur'an provides a method for resolving such disputes, one that consists of different steps designed to reach the ultimate solution in a peaceful manner. For example, Qur'an 4:34-35 outlines these steps and forbids skipping one step and going on to the next one without exhausting every possible aspect of the previous step. The Qur'an emphasizes good communication. Muslim men who abuse their wives completely neglect and misunderstand this verse. First, let's be clear that religion is never a cause of domestic violence. While Muslim men may try to justify their abuse according to this verse, the truth is that the motive for their abuse is not (and can never be) religion. How can one's relationship with God, which is the essence of religion, be a motive for harming or inflicting violence upon another human being? The causes of domestic violence are many, and experts in the field have elucidated them. Regardless of the reasons, however, we can agree that God's teachings are not one of them.

While Muslim men who are guilty of domestic violence might, in retrospect, cite 4:34 to justify their behavior, the truth is that they are attempting to skip the first two steps and jump to the third (which, nevertheless, is symbolic and not literal in its most conservative interpretation). In this regard, they ignore the general purposes of marriage in Islam, which include fulfilling the conditions needed for living in tranquility and harmony, building family relationships and networks, and procreation.

Despite the teachings and values that regulate appropriate behavior in order to prevent oppression and maltreatment, oppression occurs in all populations, including Muslim families, and exists in many forms. Victims of oppression are expected to strive to find solutions while exercising patience and forgiveness: "And those who, when an oppressive wrong is inflicted on them, (are not cowed) but help and defend themselves. The recompense for an injury is an injury equal thereto (in degree). But if a person forgives and makes reconciliation, his/her reward is due from God, for (God) loves not those who do wrong" (42:39-40). Also Qur'an 5:45 says: "We ordained therein for them: a life for a life, an eye for an eye, a nose for a nose, an ear for an ear, a tooth for a tooth, and wounds equal for equal. But if anyone remits the retaliation by way of charity, it is an act of atonement for himself. And if any fail to judge by (the light of) what God has revealed, they are (no better than) wrongdoers."

The Qur'an indicates that exercising patience and forgiveness is a positive part of the victim's healing process. Therefore, it encourages them to be strong and to seek justice without blaming themselves:

The blame is only against those who oppress people with wrongdoing and insolently transgress beyond bounds throughout the land, defying right and justice. For such (people) there will be a grievous penalty. But indeed, if any show patience and forgive, that would truly be an exercise of courageous will and resolution in the conduct of affairs. (42:42-43)

People of authority within society, such as religious leaders (e.g., imams, Muslim jurists, priests, and rabbis), should effectively push abusers to seek counsel through intervention programs, therapy, and spiritual counseling. When oppression exists anywhere, society as a whole has an obligation to interfere and prevent further abuse from occurring. Punishing people for their oppressive or unjust behavior is the responsibility of every society through its established authorities. Individuals do not have the authority to carry out the punishment as vigilantes; rather, recourse should be had to the established channels mandated and enforced by the society's legal system (Qur'an 12:1-12).

References

Abu Shaqqah, *Tahrir al-Mar'ah*, vol. 1, pp. 128-129. Dar al-Qalam, 1990.

Abugideiri, S. and Alwani, Z. (2003). *What Islam Says about Domestic Violence: A Guide for Helping Muslim Families.* Herndon, VA: FAITH.

AbuSulayman AbdulHamid, A. (2003). *Marital Discord: Recapturing the Full Islamic Spirit of Human Dignity.* London: The International Institute of Islamic Thought, p. 19.

Al Faruqi, I. (1992). *Al-Tawhid: Its Implications for Thought and Life.* Herndon, VA: International Institute of Islamic Thought. Pp. 130-133.

Alwani, Z., "The Qur'anic Model for Harmony in family relations": chapter in *Change from within: Diverse Perspectives on Domestic Violence in Muslim Communities.* Edited by Maha B. Alkhateeb & Salma Elkadi Abugideiri. Peaceful Families Project, Great Falls, VA 22066 P. 51, 2007.

Armstrong, K., *Muhammad: A Prophet for Our Time.* Atlas Books & Harper Collins Publishers, 2006. P. 147.

Asad, M., (1980), *The Message of the Qur'an.* Gibraltar: Dar al-Andalus. Cited by Asad, p. 110.

Badawi, J. (1995).*Gender Equity in Islam: Basic Principles.* Plainfield, IN: American Trust Publications.

Fath al-Bari, vol. 9, p. 249

Horley, S., "Domestic Violence: The Issue Explained." See *www.guardian. co.uk/society/2001/mar/12/6*, 2001.

Sahih Bukhari, Vol. 7, book 62, no. 132.

Jewish Perspectives in Domestic Violences

Toby Myers, Ed. D.
National Center on Domestic & Sexual Violence, Texas

In her heart she is a mourner for those who have not survived.
In her soul she is a warrior for those who are now as she was then.
In her life she is both celebrant and proof of women's capacity and
will to survive, to become, to act, to change self and society.
And each year she is stronger and there are more of her.
Andrea Dworkin 1978

Introduction

IN THIS PAPER, I posit different ideas relative to Judaism in regard to domestic violence, offer Jewish precepts and texts, raise current problems for Jewish battered women, describe Jewish programs, make known Jews in the movement/field, cite Jewish Domestic Violence cases, and conclude with Creating Rituals and Blessings.

Depending on whom one consults about the topic of Domestic Violence in the Jewish community, Naomi Graetz (1998) noted the responses may vary. Some accept and legitimize the occurrence as the exercising of the husband's inherent right to educate, discipline, and/or correct a disobedient wife. According to Jewish law, the man owns the wife. When a man is betrothed the Hebrew word *koneh* translates to the verb acquires. Some reject the concept that it is permissible for Jews to use domestic violence because of adherence to the principle that a husband is bound to honor his wife over others. That women, as well as men, are made in the image of God is a more egalitarian interpretation for rejection of domestic violence and some who respond in that way actively promote equality within Judaism. "God created man in His image, male and female, He created them," (Genesis 1:27). Some respond with denial that domestic violence occurs in Jewish families. We have heard that Jewish men make the best husbands and even

Gentile women prefer them. Some take the role of the apologist, noting that unequal and maltreatment of women occurred a long time ago when times were different, even though it became ingrained and carried over; however, they contend things are better now. Some may totally evade, using the explanation that they do not want to talk about it or it is a private matter and they are powerless to do anything to change it.

Claire Renzetti, formerly of St. Joseph's University in Pittsburgh and currently at the University of Dayton, was project director of Domestic Violence in Jewish Families in the Philadelphia Metropolitan Area. The project from 1991-1993 is thought the best and most comprehensive research on the incidence and description of Jewish domestic violence.

Wife abuse, as a social phenomenon, is maintained by the main institutions of society and religion. A change in Jewish law called *takkanah* would remedy acquisition of Jewish wives (Graetz, 1998). In the United States, civil law and religious law are separate. In religious law, a more pressing problem for Jewish women is that they are not permitted to initiate divorce. Progress toward equality and the valuing of women is noted with the ordination of women rabbis in Reconstructionist, Reform, and Conservative Judaism; however, Orthodox Judaism does not ordain women rabbis. Women have served as presidents of congregations, federations, and of other Jewish organizations.

Applicable Precepts and Texts

Landesman (2004) provided comfort based on Jewish wisdom to those who have experienced abuse.An act of *Teshuvah*, repentance and contrition, is in order for much of the Jewish community because of the state of denial regarding domestic abuse. *Teshuvah* is applicable also to those who commit the abuse. *Avadim hayyinu* recalls the one down position of Jews which is also applicable to victims, "we were slaves in Egypt," (Deuteronomy 6:221). "Do not stand idly by while your neighbor's blood is being spilled" (Leviticus 19:16) invokes Jews and the Jewish community to help those in need.

Our ancestors lived an incredibly oppressed and cruel life. God called to Moses from the burning bush and gave hope and promise. "And God said, 'I have surely seen the affliction of my people who are in Egypt and have heard their cry . . . I know their sorrows' "(Exodus 3:7) conveys to victims that someone cared.

"It is not an enemy who reviles me—I could bear that; . . . but it is you, my equal, my companion, my friend . . ." (Psalm 55:13-14) shows the understanding of problems with loved ones.

Shalom Bayit—Peace in the house, household harmony, has been the hallmark of Jewish homes and one of the few *mitzvot*, good deeds, accorded primarily to women. This can be used against women when interpreted to mean keeping the family together at any cost. Women and slaves were exempt from *mitzvot* that required something that must be done at a specific place and time. Some interpreted the exemption pejoratively as a way of restricting women. A positive interpretation viewed the exemption as a consideration to protect those needing protection or those vulnerable.

The *mitzvah* of *shalom-bayit* put women in the position of responsibility for something beyond their power to guarantee. Women who want to end the marriage with a Jewish divorce are not able to do so. A Jewish divorce or *Get* must be initiated by the husband and given to the wife. Men have been known to hold women hostages, not physically, but by not giving them a divorce. The woman is, in effect, a chained or anchored woman called an *Agunah*. Some American Jewish marriages have sought remedy by injecting the what is known as the Lieberman clause into the *Ketubah*, marriage contract, when a couple marries. The clause stipulates that divorce in civil court will also be adjudicated by a rabbinic court, *Bet Din*. Not all Judaism recognizes this strategy and some believe it treads on conflict between church and state with the religious court bound to follow the civil decision.

Jews are taught to avoid *Lashon Hara*, evil tongue or gossip, which has concomitantly been used to quiet victims, implying that talking about abuse is *Hillul Hashem*, desecration of God. Orthodox Rabbi Mark Dratch believes bringing abuse into the light, can be a *Kiddush Hashem*, honoring of God. The *Shandah*, shame or disgrace, is the abuse and tolerance thereof rather than victims being ashamed of the abuse. If *Halakha*, Jewish law, cannot protect the victim, then the law is not being interpreted correctly. Reinterpretations are more in keeping with victim perspective.

Victims draw comfort, encouragement, and support from their Judaism. *Pikuah Nefesh*, saving a life, is commanded of Jews even if the life is one's own; therefore Jewish battered women are instructed to count themselves in. Comfort is offered by G-d, "I will give you peace in the land and you will lie down, and no one will make you afraid" (Leviticus 26:6).

Humor keeps us going, "I get up. I walk. I fall down. Meanwhile, I keep dancing," attributed to Hillel.

Jewish Programs

Prominent Jewish women's organizations in the United States have worked diligently to eliminate domestic violence.

Jewish Women International (JWI), *www.jwi.org*, was founded in 1897 as an auxiliary to the men's group B'nai Brith. Since the 1990's, JWI's main focal point has been Domestic Abuse. Their website regarding Domestic Abuse is extensive and comprehensive. JWI's Legal Project Website provides information to battered women and their advocates about the legal system and other resources. JWI began hosting an International Conference on Domestic Abuse in the Jewish Community in 2003 and it continues every other year. The JWI National Alliance hosts monthly teleconferences on varied topics relevant to domestic abuse. JWI developed an education program for teens to develop healthy and non-abusive relationships. JWI's National Library Initiative collects children's books for domestic violence programs. The Mother's Day Flower Project sends flowers to mothers in shelters.

Hadassah, *www.hadassah.org*, during the Silent Witness March on Washington made sure the women from Israel killed by their husbands were represented in the event. Hadassah, a Zionist organization, is the single largest women's organization in this country and, as such, has a particular obligation and an unwavering commitment to women's rights and concerns. Hadassah has condemned all forms of violence against women including domestic violence with special emphasis on domestic violence in the Jewish community. Hadassah has called on the U. S. Government to recognize gender-based violence as grounds for asylum; adapt the asylum process to accommodate women fleeing gender-based violence, including providing female officers to hear their cases, and training immigration officers and judges on issues relating to gender-based violence; and create a high-level office within the Department of Homeland Security to oversee all issues relating to asylum and expedited removal. Hadassah has condemned the trafficking of women when women are forced, defrauded, or coerced into labor or sexual exploitation within and across national borders. Hadassah's monthly magazine has carried numerous articles on domestic violence.

National Council of Jewish Women (NCJW), *www.ncjw.org*, is a grassroots, volunteer organization that has been at the forefront of social change in the United States for over a century. Inspired by Jewish values, NCJW courageously takes a progressive stance on issues such as child welfare, women's rights, and reproductive freedom. NCJW strives for social justice

DOMESTIC VIOLENCE CROSS CULTURAL PERSPECTIVE

by improving the quality of life for women, children and families and by safeguarding individual rights and freedoms. On the grassroots level, NCJW sections around the country are involved in a variety of domestic violence prevention programs, including Court Watch programs, teen dating violence education, and Silent Witness and Clothesline projects. The organization in Houston which I helped found and develop is known as Aid to Victims of Domestic Abuse (AVDA) and was initiated by NCJW and NCJW provides continuing support. NCJW collaborates with Houston's local *Shalom Bayit* a program of Jewish Family Service, and The Bureau of Jewish Education to bring the teen domestic violence prevention program, Love Shouldn't Hurt, into Jewish religious schools.

Na'amat USA, *www.naamat.org*, for more than 80 years has had one mission: to support the women and children of Israel. To accomplish its mission, NA'AMAT—through its sister organization in Israel—provides a broad range of social services, from day care centers to domestic violence shelters.

JSafe, *www.jSafe.org*, was founded by former Orthodox pulpit rabbi Mark Dratch to set standards for training and certification of Jewish religious institutions and to hold Jewish professionals responsible in the area of domestic abuse and making sure congregations have an effective protocol for dealing with both victims and perpetrators of domestic violence.

Faith Trust Institute (FTI), *www.faithtrustinstitute.org*, is an international, multi-faith organization working to end sexual and domestic violence. FTI addresses the religious and cultural issues related to abuse. Faith Trust Institute works with many communities, including Asian and Pacific Islander, Buddhist, Jewish, Latino/a, Muslim, Black, Anglo, Indigenous, Protestant and Roman Catholic. FTI is a catalyst for change within our religious institutions and their work continues until our churches and synagogues, stakes and assemblies, mosques and temples are effectively responding to victims and abusers, bringing forth healing and justice. Religious teachings can serve as either a resource or a roadblock in addressing the issue of domestic violence. Religious communities have been aided by FTI in acting on their responsibility to minimize any barriers facing abused congregation members and maximize the resources that exist within our religious traditions. FTI (1997) produced the video about Jewish Domestic Violence, **To Save a Life**, which is available for purchase.

Jewish domestic violence shelters exist in New York. Far Rockaway, NY shelter is *kosher*. Many of the country's domestic violence programs have worked hard to meet cultural, religious, or ethnic needs of client populations. Some have partnered with religious programs for sensitivity and cultural competence activities. Jewish groups have educated domestic violence programs on anti-Semitism and Jewish cultural competence. Many domestic violence programs have the possibility for Jewish clients to keep *kosher* or at least not have pork meals. Pork is usually a problem. Domestic violence programs serve pork as it is inexpensive. Lobster and shellfish are not as problematic because of their expense. Jewish groups sometimes outfit and provide for shelters plastic trunks with non-perishable *kosher* food, prayer books, Sabbath or electric candles, separate dishes and cutlery, and other holiday items. Providing the resources has been collaborative between domestic violence programs and Jewish organizations. Shelters are not always aware a woman is Jewish as government funding does not permit programs to ask about religion. A program letting it be known that *kosher* food can me made available make services for a Jewish woman more welcoming.

Jews in the Domestic Violence Field

Two of the earliest, well-known and well-respected Jewish names in the field are Lenore Walker and Susan Schechter (of blessed memory). Best known is Walker, author of one of the first books **The Battered Woman**. Walker first described what is referred to as the Cycle of Violence comprised of the Buildup, Explosion, and Honeymoon Stages. Walker originated the term *Battered Women's Syndrome* and she has been an expert witness in many high profile cases. In her book **Women and Male Violence: The Visions and Struggles of the Battered Women's Movement**, Schechter chronicled the underpinnings, development, and challenges of early efforts against domestic violence. Much of her later work explored the way domestic violence affected children. Schechter's career was cut short by her death in 2004 from endometrial cancer. At the time of her death, she was faculty in the School of Social Work at the University of Iowa.

Paul Kivel, Gus Kaufman, Phyllis Frank, and Jackson Katz are all leaders in the work with men who are violent, abusive, and/or controlling with intimate partners. Paul Kivel, a trainer, activist, writer, and cofounder of the Oakland Men's Project, believes that violence is rooted in social injustice based on inequality in race, class, gender, and sexual orientation. Included in books authored by Kivel are **Men's Work: How to Stop the Violence that Tears our Lives Apart;** with Allan Creighton **Helping Teens Stop Violence: A Practical Guide for Counselors, Educators;** "Jewish Men and Jewish Male Violence" in **Men's Work in Preventing Violence Against Women,** editors James Poling and Christie Neuger. Gus Kaufman is one of the originators of Men Stopping Violence in Atlanta and his writings include "The Mysterious Disappearance of Battered Women in Family Therapists' Offices: Male Privilege Colluding with Male Violence" in **Secrets in Families and Family Therapy.** In 1978, Phyllis Frank designed and still directs the nationally known New York Model Program for abusive men in Rockland County, New York. Her program is part of research funded by the National Institute of Justice to assess the responsibility of the legal system for holding batterers accountable when they are not compliant with the court order to participate in and complete a battering intervention program. Anti-sexist male activist, Jackson Katz, writes, educates, and makes films in the field of gender violence prevention with men and boys, particularly in sports and the military. **The Macho Paradox: Why Some Men Hurt Women and How All Men Can Help** is his book and **Tough Guise** is his video.

Evan Stark, faculty in public administration at Rutgers University, specializes in health and medical care, family and community violence, criminal justice, and policy issues dealing with racial and gender justice. His book, **Coercive Control: How Men Entrap Women in Personal Life** reframed domestic violence as a liberty crime.

In Texas during the 1990's, six of the 12 member Texas Council on Family Violence (TCFV) Board were Jews working in domestic violence programs across the state—Fran Danis, Toby Myers, Jeff Basen-Engquist, Nina Rivkin, Rhonda Gerson, and Ellen Fisher. Fran Danis, a Professor of Social Work joined the faculty of University of Texas Arlington in August 2008. TCFV has referred to me, Toby Myers, as "the mother of the Texas Battered Women's Movement." Even though I was deeply ingrained in social justice movements, I would not have come to battered women's work had I not found myself partnered with a violent, abusive, and controlling man. I have helped to start and worked in domestic violence organizations in our city, state and nation including the first battered women's shelter in Houston and our statewide network Texas Council on Family Violence. I taught our state's the first course in Domestic Violence at Texas Woman's University in 1980.

Domestic Violence Cases Involving Jews

High profile domestic violence cases include that of Joel Steinberg and Hedda Nussbaum. On the surface, they appeared to be the epitome of an upscale, yuppie couple. He was a lawyer and she a former book editor. Photos of her when she was an editor were of a beautiful woman. Yet when their adopted daughter Lisa died from abuse and the public saw what had happened to Hedda, the myth that abuse does not exist in the Jewish community was exploded.

Steve and Elana Steinberg seemed like the perfect couple in Scottsdale, Arizona. Their home was a dream of good taste, furnished with purchases that Elana, a quintessential bargain hunter, had carefully made. In 1981, her husband stabbed her 26 times, and was acquitted by a jury after his defense attorney, also Jewish, portrayed her as a Jewish American Princess obsessed with shopping and who made incessant demands on her husband for more and better. These allegations played into the worst stereotypes of Jewish women and made inveterate gambler Steve appear the victim. The Jewish community was polarized over this case. Steinberg went to temple after his trial, acquittal, and release from jail. The rabbi granted him an *aliyah*, honor, permitting Steve's recitation of the *birkat haGomel*, the Jewish blessing of thanksgiving for one's deliverance from danger. There was no mention of Elana.

Knoxville lawyer Perry March maintained his wife Janet left one night in 1996 never to return. In 2006, March was found guilty on charges of second degree murder, tampering with evidence, and abuse of a corpse. March had been extradited to the United States from Ajijic, Mexico for arrest and trial. He, his new, Mexican wife, and his children had been living in their luxury surroundings. His own father eventually testified against him. Janet March's parents, the Levine's, worked diligently to see he was brought to justice and that their grandchildren were returned to this country. The children are with the Levines.

Cherry Hill, New Jersey Rabbi Fred Neulander was found guilty of paying hitmen to kill his wife Carol on November 1, 1994. She was found beaten to death in their home. Neulander's apparent motive was to continue a relationship with a former Philadelphia area radio personality, Elaine Soncini. He was thought to have felt a divorce would compromise his authority as a spiritual leader, and thus possibly his job; hence, the need to have his wife done away with. Suspicion swarmed around Neulander from the day of the killing, but it was not apparent who committed the actual act. Following the guilty verdict, after his second trial, Neulander was sentenced to serve 30 years to life in New Jersey State Prison. Son Matthew Neulander, now a physician, testified against him.

Jean Harris, who is not Jewish, served time in Bedford Hills for having killed Jewish Scarsdale Diet guru and high-society cardiologist Dr. Herman Tarnower. Harris, headmistress at Madeira an exclusive school in a Washington, D. C., endured fourteen years of psychological abuse and flagrant infidelity from Tarnower. Planning to take her own life in March 1980, Harris went with a gun to say goodbye to Dr. Tarnower. She ended up shooting him in a scuffle and was subsequently sentenced to prison. There, she was an ideal inmate. In 1992, Harris was granted clemency by New York Governor Mario Cuomo.

Creating Our Own Rituals and Blessings

Jews experiencing domestic violence have sought ritual and prayers specific to those needs. Sometimes the need could be fulfilled by opening a prayer book or consulting a Jewish source. Sometimes what is found does not hold the adequate words or actions for those who sought them. Consequently, women began to create their own rituals and prayers when ones that fit could not be found. Rituals and prayers were created over such milestones, both sad and happy, of miscarriage, birth, menopause, marking a same sex union, entering a child into kindergarten, buying a home, and achieving crone or wise-woman status. The Talmud teaches that one who enjoys pleasures of this world without reciting a blessing is like a thief who steals from God. Rabbis composed blessings for all imaginable events; therefore why should women not create their own special blessings and supplications? Abused women have created rituals for having survived and become freed from an abusive relationship.

A Jewish ritual should resonate something Jewish. Jewish symbols, concepts, or words may be used in a new context, but in a context that is consistent with their symbolism. For example, a *Havdalah* candle lit to separate Sabbath from the rest of the week could be lit when a child leaves home for college marking the separation from home to independence or when a divorce is obtained. A ritual is a way to sanctify changes and to make and mark a transition, to connect ourselves to past and future, and to share transitions either privately or with a larger community. Website *www.ritualwell.org* can teach how to consider, plan, develop, and carry out new rituals. Marcia Cohn Spiegel's knowledge, creativity, and commitment provided instruction on writing and developing rituals and blessings. Spiegel led many through the steps to create a ritual and or blessing. Creating a blessing starts with traditional blessing formula—1) Naming God in the formula—Blessed are Thou, Lord our God, Creator of the Universe 2) Attributes, qualities and power of God—who is great and mighty in mercy, wisdom, and loving kindness 3) Be with me as—I embark on this dangerous task of leaving this home with my children, and 4) God's ability to act—if you deem me worthy, shelter yourself over us and protect us from harm, provide us strength to perform this momentous task, and help me to be a credit and contributor to my community and to peace in the world, and help me to be a sign and example to women that they do not have to endure humiliation, control, abuse, and violence from the one with whom they should have been the most safe.

NCJW Houston more than 20 years ago initiated A Women's *Seder* Passover. Taking part in that event, Houston's *Shalom Bayit* each year includes a recitation on the empty chair in recognition of any woman not in attendance because of the oppression, control, abuse and/or violence.

Haggadot, books reciting the order of the Passover Meal have been rewritten for women, for lesbians, and for victims of domestic violence (Faith-Trust Institute's **Journey to Freedom** 2003). Rituals have been incorporated as an *Aliyah*, an honor given during the Jewish services, for having freed oneself and having survived an abusive relationship. During the portion of the regular Service, many rabbi's when reciting the *Mi She'Beyrach* special prayer for the sick and afflicted, include battered women. Important, not only because it has a message for victims that they are not alone, but also it is a sign in the community that an important religious institution takes a position and stands with those who are victims.

It is essential that the Jewish Community, in recognition of Jewish battered women, partner with them to assure that their voices are heard in all their richness and that a milieu is created that disallows violence, abuse, and control and that promotes equality and true peace in the home. As that occurs, women will keep moving toward full status and participation in all phases of the Jewish community. Work toward that end has happened. More is needed. More is underway. More will come. Those who have been part of the effort will derive satisfaction in knowing our contribution meant something.

References

Journey towards freedom: A *haggadah* for women who have experienced domestic violence. (2003). Seattle, WA: *Faith Trust Institute. www. faithtrustinstitute.org.*

Frondorf, S. (1988). *Death of a "Jewish American princess:" The true story of a victim on trial.* New York: Villard Books.

Gerson, R. & Myers, T. (1988 June). Abuse in Jewish families. *Lilith,* 20:6-9.

Graetz, N. (1998). *Silence is deadly: Judaism confronts wifebeating.* New York: Jason Aronson.

Jacobs, L. & Dimarsky, S. B. (1991-2 Winter) Jewish domestic abuse: Realities and responses. *Journal of Jewish Communal Service, 68(2),* 94-113.

Landesman, T. (2004). *You are not alone: Solace and inspiration for domestic violence survivors based on Jewish wisdom.* Seattle, WA: Faith Trust Institute.

Lockhart, L. & Danis, F. (in press). *Domestic violence intersectionality: Culturally competent practice with diverse populations.* New York: Columbia University Press.

Mekudeshet: Sentenced to marriage (2004). 65 minute documentary (Hebrew with subtitles, director Anat Zuria). Israel: AmithosFilms.

Myers, T. (2000). Book review of Naomi Graetz's Silence is deadly: Judaism confronts wifebeating. *Violence Against Women,* 6(9), 332-334.

Spiegel, M. C. (1994). Old Symbols, New Rituals: Adapting Traditional Symbols, Ceremonies, and Blessings. *http://www.ritualwell.org/lifecycles/ primaryobject. 2005-11-16.2926929096.*

Spitzer, J. R. (1995). *When love is not enough: Spousal abuse in rabbinic and contemporary Judaism.* New York: Women of Reform Judaism, Federation of Temple Sisterhoods.

To save a life: Ending domestic violence in Jewish families (1997). A 35 minute DVD, study guide, and brochure. Seattle, WA: Faith Trust Institute. *www.faithtrustinstitute.org.*

Twerski, A. (1997). *The Shame borne in silence: Spouse abuse in the Jewish community.* Pittsburgh: Mirkov, 1997.

Walker, L. (1997). Jewish Battered Women: *Shalom Bayit* or a *Shonde?* In R. Josefowitz Seigel and E. Cole (Eds), *Celebrating the lives of Jewish women: Patterns in a feminist sampler.* New York: Haworth Press.

Weitzman, S. (2000). *Not to people like us: Hidden abuse in upscale marriages.* New York: Basic Books.

The Hindu/Indian Woman and Domestic Violence

Avayam Ramani, L.M.S.W.

S ASHIKALA (NOT HER real name), affectionately called Sashi by her family, stood alone on the backyard patio one winter night. The chilly Dallas wind blew, moving the hair out of her face, but it could not stop the warm tears from flowing down her cheeks. The thin night dress made her shiver. She rubbed her elbows to keep warm, but quickly moved them as they touched the fresh bruises from her fall when her husband had pushed her out and locked the door. She bit her lips to try and stop herself from crying, but knew that nobody would hear her even if she cried out loud. She did not know how long she stood there, until she suddenly heard her six-month-old son crying from inside. She hurriedly wiped her tears and banged on the doors for her husband to let her in. Through the window, she could see him shaking the baby in order to end his crying. Worried that her husband would harm the boy in anger, she started to bang on the door more vigorously. Her husband, irritated by the crying and banging, opened the door and pulled her in with the baby in his hands. As Sashi reached out for the crying baby, her husband grabbed her hand and said: "Promise that you will behave. Say sorry for not opening the door right away when I came home from work." Sashi said all of the above, got her son, and calmed him down.

The next morning, after her husband left for work, Sashi told her friend about the incident. The friend urged her to call the police, seek medical help, and inform her own family. But Sashi declined to do any of that, saying that: "For my child's sake, I need to stay in this marriage" and went on to say that it is her karma. "I must have done something wrong in my previous life," she continued. "As a Hindu woman, I should follow a wife's dharma [duty]."

What is Sashi talking about? What are karma and dharma? To understand these, we should have some knowledge about Indian culture in general and Hinduism in particular. There are many theories about the origin of Hinduism, the world's oldest religion. The majority of Indians are Hindus.

Given that it is considered a way of life, a Hindu is expected to practice his/her religion in everyday life. Logic and reason play an important role, but if there is no transcendental experience, then they have no place. Thus, Hinduism paves the way for one to experience and contemplate on the ability to obtain enlightenment, therefore becoming spiritually evolved. The religion's uniqueness is its belief in reincarnation and karma. (These beliefs are also present in other Indian religions like Buddhism.)

VEDAS

Hindus believe that the Vedas (the "books of knowledge'), Hinduism's authoritative scriptures, Vedas are eternal and stand for nothing less than divine truthfulness. The great sage Veda Vyasa collected, edited, and wrote them down in four volumes. To master these hymns, one requires vigorous training and practice. Vedas are non-gender specific.

THE UPANISHADS

The Upanisads, literally meaning "to sit near (upa) in a devoted manner (nisad)," indicates the process of a disciple learning earnestly from a guru/ spiritual master. These texts consist of elaborate, intensive guidelines on how to obtain knowledge about the Vedas, Vedic culture, and philosophy. Nobody knows how many Upanisads existed, but 108 of them have been preserved. These are the works of saints and seers who were not builders of systems, but rather recorders of experience. Most of the Upanishads are in a question and answer format, which encourages disciples to think, contemplate, and seek clarification from the guru. There were many gurukulams (guru's place), each defining their own path to attain enlightenment.

One such sage was Manu, who is revered as the person who passed on the codes of humanity called the Laws of Manu (Manu Dhrama Sastra). Some scholars think that these date back to 600 BC. Tradition says that they contain about 100,000 verses; however, only about 4,000 verses are available today. They cover approximately twelve chief topics, one of which is gruha dharma (marriage and the duties of family members). This topic describes the moral and ethical responsibilities of each household member.

All of these laws were meant to keep social order, and while they should not be compared to modern laws, they did pertain to the socio-religious culture of ancient times. Here is one such law: "There is no such thing as divorce. A woman who leaves her husband should be shunned. No other man can marry her." This and similar codes, all of which restricted a married woman, were passed on for centuries and generations. In fact, the current Hindu Marriage Act was based on this. It took many reformers and advocates to modernize the law. However, the majority of women, brought up with these codes ingrained in their minds, have had very difficult time getting empowered to change.

The Puranas (mythological stories) also adhere to the Manu Dhrama Sastra. Women who stepped out of those boundaries were punished, ill treated, and shunned by society.

Sashi was brought up with these ideas. She is worried that if she leaves her husband, she will be blamed for the break-up and her son will grow up without a father; that no one will believe her, because her husband is well educated and has a respectable and good-paying job; and that she will be guilty of not following her dharma. What she fails to understand, however, is that her husband is also bound by these dharmas, which tell him to respect, protect, and nurture his wife.

DHARMA

Dharma means performing one's duty. Hinduism institutes four orders of duty, each with a definite set of expectations: the spiritual man, the warrior, the trader, and the laborer. These orders have obligatory duties according to the staples of a person's growth: the student, the householder, the person retired from active life, and the monk. In ancient Hindu culture, these ways of life were distinct and sharply defined. In modern times, though, these rights and duties have been. This is why Sahsi thinks that it is her duty as wife to take no action against her abusive husband. Yet she fails to understand that as a human being, she has the right to take appropriate actions that would bring about a better outcome in the long run.

KARMA

Karma basically states that you reap what you sow. It is the theory of cause and effect. According to it, our birth and whatever happens afterward are the result of our past lives. So, she believes that her karma put her in this abusive situation and that it is her duty to go through it in order to release herself from its chains so that she can obtain salvation. But she fails to understand that her husband has a duty to respect and honor another human being, be it his wife, child, parents, or others.

REINCARNATION

Hindus believe in reincarnation, which is defined as each person being reborn many, many times (not necessarily as a human being) in order to evolve and attain enlightenment/salvation. To be born as a human being is the highest order, for there, one has the opportunity to meditate, contemplate, explore, and experience the inner self; in other words, to achieve oneness with God. Also, it is an opportunity to get rid of past sins and accumulate good deeds. Sashi thinks that her present condition is an opportunity to rid herself of past sins through suffering, as opposed to this being an opportunity for her to help somebody else to evolve as a better human being, namely, making her husband understand that his cruelty and abuse will only harm him. With a long history of advanced civilization, as long as Hindu women adhered to their duties as daughters, wives, and mothers, they enjoyed a high status. They had the freedom to choose their husbands, hold high governmental positions, and were well respected in society. But that all changed when India fell under the invasions and occupations from the west. In order to protect their women from these foreign warriors, men began to marry them off at young ages. Gradually, women became socially and economically dependent upon the male head of the household. The resulting socioeconomic dependency diminished women's rights to think and act freely. For example, their marriages were arranged. One of the ills stemming from this was giving dowry (money and jewels). Marring off daughters thus became a burden. In addition, women sometimes suffered abuse by living in a joint-family arrangement in which they may not have had a chance to voice their opinions. They endured all this because they believed it was their dharma and karma.

All of the above started to change as social activists began to fight for woman's rights. Many Indian women are now well-educated, economically independent, and have the right to vote. In addition, the government has enacted many programs to empower them, as well as an act to end child marriage. Women have the right to go to family court to obtain a divorce and can no longer be forced into a marriage, giving and receiving a dowry is against the law, and anyone can be charged with domestic abuse. But despite these laws, policies, and advancements, many Hindu women continue to suffer domestic abuse in silence in the name of dharma and karma due to their misconceptions about Hindu teachings and clinging to old beliefs in modern times. They carry this value and belief with them wherever they live.

Hindu women need to become aware of their power. They need to break all of the barriers, challenge their community and society to make them understand that domestic violence is not accepted in any form, and to use the available resources. In this way, they can take one step forward, however small it may be. Doing this will constitute a giant step for womankind.

The Effects of Domestic Violence on Children

Rosalyn Hubbard, M.S.S.W., B.S.W., B.C.J.

L IKE THE CYCLE of violence, the effect of domestic violence flows endlessly and bounds us all. Studies have validated that there is a significant correlation between child and domestic abuse. A 1990 Massachusetts Department of Social Services review of 200 substantiated child abuse reports found domestic violence occurred in 30 percent of the cases. Dykstra & Alsop more recent studies found the number has now elevated to 48 percent, (Adoption, 2008). A review of Washington State CPS cases found 55 percent of the emotional and physical abuse referrals also involved domestic violence, and 47 percent of the referrals involving only emotional abuse of children co-existed with domestic violence (Adoption, 2008).

In the medical setting, where the most detrimental forms of child abuse or neglect were treated, a soaring occurrence of domestic violence coexisted. Stark and Flitcraft (1988) found in a study of 116 children suspected of being abused or neglected, Forty-five percent of the mothers' previous medical records that indicated domestic violence/abuse. McKibben, De Vos, and Newberger (1989) repeated the Stark and Flitcraft study at a Boston hospital and found 59 percent of mothers of child abuse/neglect victims had medical histories indicated they had been victims of domestic violence (Adoption, 2008). More than 400 battered women found 28 percent of them abused their children while residing with an abusive partner and 6 percent made threats of abuse to their children. In addition, 5 percent of them physically abused their children when irritated or angered by the abusive partner (Adoption, 2008). Ross (1996) found in a group of female batterers, 24 percent also abused their children. "These rates are higher than child abuse rates of parents who were not violent toward each other (Adoption, 2008).

The correlation between child maltreatment and domestic violence is documented in non-clinical situations as well. The National Family Violence Survey involving over 3,000 American parents interviewed for the 1985

(Straus & Gelles, 1986) found 23 percent of the male batterers also were perpetrators of child abuse as well. In this study, the more incidents of domestic violence increased the acts of child maltreatment by 12 percent on average (Adoption, 2008). Studies indicate that where either child maltreatment or domestic violence occured the other form of violence also exist (WEAVE, 2008).

- Child abuse and domestic violence are linked in a number of important ways that have serious consequences for the safety of children (Place, 2007)
- Studies of abused children in the general population reveal that nearly half of them have mothers who are also abused, making wife abuse the single strongest identifiable risk factor for child abuse (Newton, Domestic Violence: An Overview. Effects of Domestic Violence on Children and Teenagers., 2001).
- The rate of child abuse is from six to fifteen times higher in families where the mother is abused compared to families where the mother is not abused (WEAVE, 2008).
- Many battered women report that their abuser threaten or attack the children as a way to control and hurt the mothers even more (WEAVE, 2008).
- Of women coming to shelters, more than half report that their children are also physically, emotionally and sometimes sexually abused; the child abuser is two to three times more likely to be the woman's abuser than the battered woman herself (WEAVE, 2008).
- In approximately half of the families experiencing domestic violence, there is physical and verbal child abuse (WEAVE, 2008).
- Children who witness domestic abuse have significantly higher levels of behavioral and emotional problems than other children (WebMD, 2006).

The Child Witness

Domestic Violence can affect the quality of care as well as the quantity of time spent with the child. Parents often state and believe that they are able to hide the abuse/violence from their children. Research suggests that between 80 and 90 percent of these children are aware of the violence (Fund, 2008).

When a parent is abused the child often feel's the atmosphere becoming more strained as the batterer escalates his behavior and witnesses the violence as it happens either by sight or sound. Most children are able to provide detailed accounts of the abuse. If nothing else the child also experiences the aftermath of the violence (Fund, 2008).

Exposure to domestic violence increases the chance of the children being abused themselves either by accident while observing, or purposely when either the batterer or the adult victim deals with the child while under stress caused by the violence. Younger children are especially at risk as they are hit while being held by the adult victim or assaulted by objects thrown with little to no concern for the child's safety. Studies even suggest, "Battered women may use more punitive child-rearing strategies or exhibit aggression toward their children." This over disciplining of the children usually occurs the adult victim feels the need to gain control of the children's behavior in an effort to protect them from greater abuse that would be inflicted by the batterer. Domestic violence emotionally and physically impairs everyone involved, especially children (WEAVE, 2008). Older children become targets for abuse while attempting to rescue the adult victim. "Many children are further victimized by coercion to remain silent about the abuse, maintaining the "family secret (Fund, 2008)."

In contrast, abused victims may also neglect their children, giving all their attention the batterer. Usually this is done to "make the batterer happy" thus attempting to control reoccurrence or the level of violence. It may also occur in response to the fears of the adult victim. Researchers Rossman and Rosenberg have concluded that exposure to domestic violence is child abuse (Adoption, 2008).

Outcomes for Children

Society suffers as the result of domestic violence. The population that is affected the greatest from domestic violence are children. Children witnessing domestic violence can lead to many negative outcomes. As stated above these children have exaggerated risk factors and are exposed to abuse and neglect on many levels. Children suffer both directly and indirectly and in all areas of development at various stages of growth. Studies have found three consistent categories of childhood problems directly associated with witnessing domestic violence (Fund, 2008). Category one is the "**Behavioral, social, and emotional problems**: higher levels of aggression, anger, hostility, oppositional behavior, and disobedience; fear, anxiety, withdrawal, and depression; poor peer, sibling, and social relationships; low self-esteem (Fund, 2008)." Category two "**Cognitive and attitudinal problems**: lower cognitive functioning, poor school performance, lack of conflict resolution skills, limited problem-solving skills, acceptance of violent behaviors and attitudes, belief in rigid gender stereotypes and male privilege (Fund, 2008)." Category three "**Long-term problems**: higher levels of adult depression and trauma symptoms, increased tolerance for and use of violence in adult relationships (Fund, 2008)."

These problems can be better identified when looking at behaviors associated with the different stages of childhood.

Pre-natal:

> Studies show a much higher rate of miscarriages among woman who are battered while they are pregnant than woman who are not. It is also believed that severe battering can be responsible for some birth defects and or malformations of the fetus.

Infants:

> Battering and domestic violence need not take place directly upon the infant in order to affect them. Just by being subjected to the type of environment in which there may be frequent fighting, yelling, arguing and or screaming causes excessive crying and irritability, sleep disturbance, digestive problems.

Toddlers & Preschoolers:

> It can cause children who witness it to be more aggressive than other children or more withdrawn than other children; difficulty learning, delays in verbal development, poor motor skills, general fearfulness, anxiety, stomach aches, nightmares; lack of bowel and bladder control in children over 3 years of age, lack of confidence to begin new tasks.

Elementary & Middle School Aged Children:

> Poor grades, or in special classes (SLD, EH), failure on one or more grade levels; poor social skills, low self esteem, general aggressiveness, violent outbursts of anger, bullying or withdrawn, dependent, bed wetting, nightmares.

Teenagers & Young adults:

> Poor grades, failure in school, quits school altogether, low self esteem, refuses to bring friends home, stays away from home or feels responsible to take care of home and mother, runaway, violent outbursts of anger, destroying property, poor judgment, irresponsible decision making, unable to communicate feelings, immaturity, withdrawn, few friends, nightmares, bed wetting, dating violence and joins in on physical abuse with parent.

Source: (Nevada Urban Indians, 2008)

Misdiagnosis

The effects of domestic violence on children also illustrate how their reactions can mimic so-called diagnosable disorders, including attention deficit/hyperactivity disorder. These reactions can be exaggerated in crisis situations, such as when a child is temporarily residing in a domestic violence shelter, and should be considered normal responses to abnormal situations.

Most child witnesses exhibit symptoms that closely resemble Post Traumatic Stress Disorder (PSTD) or sleep deprivation. The children have aggressive behaviors, short attention spans, hyper vigilance, and are distracted easily. Witnessing the physical, emotional, financial, and mental abuse of the person they depend on for support and love while having to helplessly standby can be traumatic. Often times the children are unable to suffer from a lack of sleep due to the fear of what may happen when and if they go to sleep. The children feel helpless or afraid because they are unable to protect the abused parent or even themselves from the batterer's behavior (Womenspace, 2008).

The Question of Loyalty

Child witnesses are exposed to so many forms of abuse. The children may be used as a spy to find out information from the adult victim, a wager by the abuser to coerce the adult victim to perform particular behaviors or to return to the abusive relationship. Children have also been forced to watch and/or participate in the abuse of the adult victim in return for the child's safety.

Physical as well as emotional injury often occurs as a result. In other instances the children suffer abuse directly by the batterer in an attempt to control the adult victim. This is unmistakably child maltreatment (Fund, 2008). Some children might also lose respect for their mother—and a woman in general—if their mother's abuser constantly tells her she is worthless and unable to care for her children. Emotionally the children must contend with conflicting emotions about a batterer they often both fear and love.

The Cycle

Domestic violence and child abuse are usually learned behaviors. A 1983 study in Baltimore found ". . . 75% of men seen in a batterer's program reported witnessing their fathers' abuse their mothers-50% reported being abused as children (Womenspace, 2008)." Children take what they see and apply it to their lives many times over. According to the Journal of Interpersonal Violence, "abusers are six times more likely to have seen their fathers beating their mothers than non-abusers (one study showed 45% of abusers had seen their mothers abused as compared to 7.5% of non-abusers.) And almost 82% of those boys witnessing spouse abuse were also abused themselves, thus confirming a strong relationship between spouse abuse and child abuse (Womenspace, 2008)."

"Some studies have indicated that adults who witnessed violence in the home as children were significantly more likely to engage in interpersonal aggression, and to remain in an abusive relationship. In particular, the males in these studies-expressed an attitude of approval regarding wife abuse and were less able to resolve conflict situations constructively. Witnessing domestic violence as a child has been identified by sociologists and social learning theorists as the most common risk factor for becoming abusive towards a wife or lover in adulthood (Womenspace, 2008)."

Domestic violence and child abuse often represented or explained using a circle to represent what it is . . . a cycle with no beginning or end unless there is interruption.

The Solution

The most effective solution would be for all forms of family violence to be nonexistent. However, until this goal is reached, effective intervention will require a more coordinated response to child abuse and domestic violence by battered women advocates, child protective workers, judges and community members to help keep families safer (Fund, 2008).

Help society help children by reporting suspected abuse.

Two Ways to Report Abuse in Texas

Via phone

- ◉ 1-800-252-5400
  Call the Texas Department of Health Abuse Hotline toll-free 24 hours a day, 7 days a week, nationwide.

Via Website

- ◉ www.txabusehotline.org
  Make your report through their secure web site and you will receive a response within 24 hours.
- ◉ https://reportabuse.ws/swilogin.asp
  Professional Reporting Website
  Log in: professional
  Password: report1

Texas Department of Human Services cannot accept e-mail reports of suspected abuse or neglect.

State Crisis Hot Lines

State	Phone	State	Phone
Alabama	334 793-5214	Nebraska	800 876-6238
Alaska	907 586-3650	Nevada	800 500-1556
Arizona	602 279-2900 800 782-6400	New York, English: New York, Spanish:	800 942-6906 800 942-6908
Arkansas	501 663-4668	New Mexico	800 773-3645
California, Central California, Southern	209 524-1888 310 655-6098	New Jersey	800 572-7233
Colorado	303 573-9018	New Hampshire	800 852-3388

Connecticut	203 524-5890	North Dakota	800 472-2911
Delaware	800 701-0456	North Carolina	919 956-9124
District of Columbia	202 783-5332	Ohio	800 934-9840
Florida	904 668-6862	Oklahoma	800 522-9054
Georgia	800 643-1212	Oregon	503 223-7411
Hawaii	808 486-5072	Pennsylvania	800 932-4632
Idaho	208 384-0419	Puerto Rico	809 722-2907
Illinois	800 241-8456	Rhode Island	800 494-8100
Indiana	800 332-7385	South Carolina	800 260-9293
Iowa	800 942-0333	South Dakota	605 225-5122
Kansas	913 232-9784	Tennessee	800 356-6767
Kentucky	502 875-4132	Texas	800 252-5400
Louisiana	800 837-5400	Utah	801 538-4100
Maine	207 941-1194	Utah	801 538-4100
Maryland	800 634-3577	Vermont	802 223-1302
Massachusetts	617 248-0922	Virginia	800 838-8238
Michigan	517 484-2924	Washington	800 562-6025
Minnesota	800 646-0994	West Virginia	304 765-2250
Mississippi	601 981-9196	Wisconsin	608 255-0539
Missouri	314 634-4161	Wyoming	800 990-3877
Montana	406 256-6334		

Source: (Nevada Urban Indians)

References

Adoption.com (2008). "In Harm's Way: Domestic Violence and Child Maltreatment." Retrieved August 5, 2008 from *http://library.adoption.com/Child-Safety/In-Harms-Way-Domestic-Violence-and-Child-Maltreatment/article/3519/1.html*.

Family Prevention Fund (2008). "The Effects of Domestic Violence on Children." Retrieved May 23, 2008 from http://endabuse.org/programs/display.php3?DocID=150.

Nevada Urban Indians, Inc., (n.d.). "The Effects of Domestic Violence on Children. Retrieved May 23, 2008 from www.nevadaurbanindians.org/the_effects_of_domestic_violence_on_children.htm.

Newton, C. (2001, February). "Domestic Violence: An Interview. Crisis-line and Hotlines." Retrieved May 23, 2008 from www.findcounseling.com/journal/domestic-violence/domestic-violence-children.html.

Newton, C. (2001, February). "Domestic Violence: An Overview. Effects of Domestic Violence on Children and teenagers." Retrieved May 23, 2008 from www.nevadaurbanindians.org/the_effects_of_domestic_violence_on_children.htm.

Place, A. S. (2007). "Effects of Domestic Violence on Children: Part 1." Retrieved May 23, 2008 from www.asafeplaceforhelp.org/childrendomesticviolence.html.

Programs, W. R. (n.d.). "The Effects of Domestic Violence on Children." Retrieved May 23, 2008, from www.letswrap.com/dvinfo/kids.htm.

WEAVE 2008, Inc. (n.d.). "Effects of Domestic Violence on Children." Retrieved May 23, 2008 from www.WEAVE, 2008inc.org/domesticviolence/children.

WebMD. (2006, April 14). "Domestic Violence: Harmful Effects of Domestic Violence." Retrieved May 23, 2008 from www.webmd.com/balance/tc/domestic-violence-harmful-effects-of-domestic-violence.

Womenspace (2008). "The Effects of Domestic Violence on Children." Retrieved August 5, 2008 from *http://youth.enddomesticviolence.org/my parents%5CEffectsonchildrenFromOregonProtocolHandbook.asp*.

An Introduction to Family Violence Prosecution with Consideration of the Diverse Victim Population

Erin Hendricks, Prosecutor

FAMILY VIOLENCE ENCOMPASSES a range of crimes against another person. The Texas Family Code considers family violence to include violence against a family member, a dating partner (or ex-dating partner), and others in the same household. Violent acts include any acts or threats against such persons that are intended to result in physical harm, bodily injury, assault, sexual assault, or any threat that puts the person in fear of the above. Violence does not have to be physical. Not all victims are necessarily cooperative with prosecution, but the State has a duty to protect those who cannot or will not protect themselves. As prosecutors, we act to hold offenders accountable and keep victims—current and future—safe from violence at the hands of an intimate partner or family member.

Why the State Prosecutes Domestic Violence Cases

The State prosecutes offenders, even if it may be against the victim's wishes, in order to protect the victim, the children, and the community. Enforcement of the law functions to make society a better place for everyone.

The State prosecutes for the victim. The primary reason for women's visits to hospital emergency rooms is domestic violence. Victims go to the emergency room with cracked orbital bones, dislocated jaws, fractured spines, and in need of stitches, medication, and help. Domestic violence has an effect beyond the injuries; approximately one-half of all homeless women are homeless due to domestic violence. On any given day, more than three women are murdered by their significant other during a domestic dispute. They are beaten to death, suffocated, strangled, or shot.

Children are an innocent group harmed by domestic violence. It is not out of the ordinary for there to be threats, yelling, and physical abuse in the home. Over one million children a year witness domestic violence, and it is something they will carry with them for the rest of their lives. Sadly, domestic violence can become a part of who they are and how they view the world. It is important to consider the greater affect on the children. Of course, witnessing domestic violence causes them fear and anxiety—but consider the greater, more far-reaching effects. They can act out, withdraw, wet the bed, and otherwise express (manifestly or not) their negative reactions to domestic violence.

Domestic violence also harms the community. Eighty-five percent of all men aged 18 to 23 in the Texas Department of Corrections grew up in a violent home. Witnessing domestic violence taught them how to interact with others in society. The domestic violence with which they were raised affected society: innocent people suffered, and society as a whole pays. It has to pay to keep individuals in prison, for police and court costs, for foster care and shelters, as well as for sick leave, absenteeism, and lost productivity. Excluding the costs of housing inmates in the prison systems, family violence costs the United States $5-10 billion per year. In the end, we all pay for domestic violence.

Many times the victim will not want to prosecute. She will state this explicitly and/or recant or change her story and attempt to blame herself or say nothing happened. After calling the police, filing a report, and getting the batterer taken away to jail, a victim may still recant. This can be for a variety of reasons, from fear to love. The victim may still be under the abuser's influence or afraid that he will get out of jail and make life harder on her. A batterer may convince the victim that she needs him in order to survive, and that living with him is her only option. Love for the batterer will allow the victim to convince herself that he will change. She may even feel responsible for the event, which she has learned from the batterer constantly telling her that it is her fault that he acts that way, or that if she would only do things right he would not get angry and blow up at her. Family and religious pressure can also cause a victim to stay with the batterer and change her story in hopes of halting the prosecution. These supposed support networks can also convince the victim that it is her fault. This combination of factors can make a victim feel trapped and lead her to recant or withdraw from the prosecution.

The Advocate's Role

The role of an advocate in the criminal justice system is to bridge the gap between the victim and the prosecutor, helping each one get the information she needs. In any client interaction, safety is the primary issue. This can include helping the victim create an emergency response plan, move to a safer location, or obtain a protective order. Safety plans are a crucial part of dealing with family violence. A plan will include an outline of key phrases that will signal someone to call for help, safe places to go, where children should go if they are present, and how they plan to handle such situations in the future.

Advocates are more than safety planners; they are a support for the complainant. An advocate may be the only person with whom the victim feels she can speak and be open about what really happened, her concerns, and how she wants the issue to be handled. Thus, he/she needs to be supportive and send positive messages to the victim. Each advocate should let the victim know that what happened is not her fault. Victims need reassurance that someone out there cares about their safety and knows that they did not deserve this. A variety of resources exist for victims of family violence, and advocates can explain these programs and help the victims get through the situation. While facing a person who went back to her violent household, it may be hard not to judge, for we are there to protect them, even if they are unable to protect themselves.

The relationship between an advocate and a victim lives on beyond the time of disposition. An advocate's role begins during the police investigation. Victims need someone to whom they can talk and who can help them throughout the legal process from the very beginning. It is a stressful and confusing time for everyone involved in the situation, and being thrown into the legal arena without someone there to explain what is going on makes it even more difficult. An advocate continues to assist the victim during the initial review by the assistant district attorney assigned to the case. At this point, the advocate is the voice of the victim to the prosecutor: conveying the victim's wishes, looking out for the victim, and conveying the status of the case to the victim for the prosecutor.

During plea-bargaining, the advocate is there to explain the process to the victim and ensure that she is comfortable with the agreement. The victim can provide insights about the offender, assist in the plea-bargaining process, and aid in the resolution. A victim of domestic violence often knows the offender better than the State, and the victim is an essential part of the entire process. If the case proceeds to trial, advocates are necessary to help the victim prepare for trial, be a support for the victim during the trial, and speak with the victim after trial about the resolution of the case. Win or lose, an advocate's duty includes ensuring that the situation is safe.

Safety Tools in Family Violence Cases

An emergency protective order (EPO) may be issued after an offense involving family violence for thirty to ninety days. An EPO can be issued if the alleged perpetrator is in jail for a family violence offense (e.g., sexual assault and stalking) and if the victim, the State's attorney, a police officer, or a magistrate requests one. Applying for an EPO is mandatory if the offense involves either serious bodily injury or a deadly weapon. The police, the district attorney's office, or the victim may seek an EPO in order to provide immediate relief or assurance to victims of family violence. In such a case, a judge or magistrate orders the offender to stay away from the victim's home and work site and to commit no further violence (including threats or harassment), among other conditions. An EPO is police enforceable.

A victim in a family violence case can seek a "permanent" (two-year) protective order. This can also be sought when there is a qualifying family violence relationship and previous acts of violence or threats of imminent bodily injury, the most recent incident occurring within ninety days of the application. Unlike restraining orders, protective orders authorize police action any time the order is violated. After the victim has applied and before the order has been issued, if there is a clear and present danger of family violence, a temporary ex parte protective order can be issued and is valid for period not to exceed twenty days (it can, however, be extended for additional twenty-day periods), if it is signed within twenty-four hours by the judge. Temporary ex parte orders are police enforceable if the offender/respondent is served with the order.

A final protective order prevents the offender (respondent) from committing family violence against the applicant/victim, communicating directly with the applicant/victim in a threatening or harassing manner, communicating a threat through any person to the applicant/victim, going to or being within 500 feet of the residence of the applicant/victim, going to or being within 500 feet of the place of employment or business of the applicant/victim, and possessing a firearm (unless, of course, the person is a peace officer actively engaged in employment as a sworn, full-time paid employee of a state agency or a political subdivision). (Note: a victim of sexual assault may also seek a final protective order, regardless of the relationship with the offender.)

During the pendency of a criminal case, bond modifications may be used to keep the offender in jail until the case can be disposed. Prosecutors can move to hold a bond insufficient and show that it should be increased or removed all together by demonstrating to the court the offender's violent nature, the victim's fears, and the likelihood that the offender would return to abuse again if he was out on bond. Under the Texas Code of Criminal Procedure Article 17.152, a violator of a protective order or other special condition of bond (like a stay away order) may be denied bond. (This law allows judges to deny bond for any offender who violates, whether he is a first-time offender or a serial offender.) A stay away or no contact order as a condition of the bond requires the offender to stay away from the victim at all times. This would prohibit the batterer from contacting the victim in any way: in person, by phone, through letters or a third party, and so on. There is no contact whatsoever allowed while a no contact order is in effect.

An electronic leg monitor (ELM) can be used to track the offender's location while not in custody. An ELM ensures to the court that the offender is not going within a certain distance of the victim (at her home and/or work). It is an effective safety tool for monitoring high-risk offenders and ensuring the victims' safety (and peace of mind) while a case awaits disposition (or during an offender's probation after disposition of the case).

Finally, during the pendency of the criminal matter, a victim may choose to sign an affidavit of non-prosecution (ANP). In some cases, the victim only wants to "drop charges" and does not change her story or recant. Often, she will change her story and make the offender appear innocent for a variety of reasons, including the fact that she still loves him or he has forced her to sign the affidavit. It is hard for the victim to understand, but the presence of an affidavit for non-prosecution does not stop the case from moving forward. The affidavit serves as a vehicle for the complainant to give her story again and let the State know how she feels about the matter being pursued. Although the victim may not want (or at least says she does not want) the case to continue, the State assesses the case as it sees fit. At this point, it is not the victim against the offender, but the State bringing charges against the offender.

Disposing of a Criminal Case

In the majority of cases, the State will carry the case on until its final disposition. The defendant may enter a plea of guilty or not guilty. A plea of guilty can result in what is commonly referred to as an agreed plea, an open plea, or a slow plea. An agreed plea is an agreement reached between the prosecution and defense to which the defendant has also agreed. A defendant may plead guilty to the alleged offense or to a lesser included offense, as agreed to by the State. This agreement can be anything from probation to prison time, depending upon the severity of the offense, the circumstances, and the defendant's criminal history. Open pleas are guilty pleas by the defendant who chooses to go to court for sentencing. Slow pleas involve the defendant pleading guilty to the alleged crime, but again he does not agree to a sentence. In a slow plea, the defendant chooses to be sentenced by a jury.

A not guilty plea brings about the commencement of a trial, whether it is before a jury or the court. The defendant has a constitutional right to a jury trial; however, he may waive that right to be judged and sentenced by the bench. If the defendant chooses a jury trial, he will go to trial before a jury of twelve individuals. Although the State carries the burden to prove the defendant's guilt, either the prosecution or the defense may provide evidence regarding the defendant's guilt or innocence, and then the jury will deliberate and find the defendant guilty or not guilty. If the jury finds the defendant guilty, the trial enters the second stage, during which both sides may present more evidence regarding aggravating and mitigating factors for sentencing. After the testimony is over, the jury deliberates again and pronounces a sentence that falls within the required sentencing range as prescribed by law. (See Quick Reference Guide, attached.)

A Focus on Diverse Victim Populations

An immigrant woman may seem an easy target to her abuser due to her non-citizen status in the United States. A batterer will gain leverage over and use tactics to intimidate and control the victim. Culture plays a role; many women believe that an abusive situation is normal, since they grew up seeing it in their home and community. Furthermore, as a non-citizen, a victim might feel that she has fewer rights and privileges and not realize that she has access to legal services. Sometimes, immigrant victims feel that they will be deported, lose their children, or that the law will not care if they do report the violence; in other words, that their pleas for help will be ignored. The batterer may threaten the victim with deportation in order to have more power over her or convince her that if she does report anything, they will both be in trouble. Such misperceptions of the system puts a victim in what she feels is a no-win situation.

Diverse victim populations pose additional issues for prosecutors and advocates to keep in mind when evaluating and working on a case. We all recognize that cultures differ in a variety of ways, and we cannot forget these differences when dealing with victims of family violence. By familiarizing ourselves with the practices of different cultures, we may be better able to understand the victims, the aggressors, and the dynamics of their relationships. Many cultures maintain traditional roles for husbands and wives: who holds the power, how they interact, who dominates household decisions, and what factors influence how household decisions are made. Working with a victim, we must start where the victim is. We cannot assume that the victim has assimilated into American culture and operates within it comfortably. Knowledge of community resources located within the individuals' comfort zone may help us to understand the victim.

Also, familiarity with matters related to immigration and citizenship better equips a prosecutor or advocate to assist the victim and make her feel more comfortable with you and the situation. A victim may be eligible for U Visa Interim Relief if four basic eligibility requirements are met: (1) The immigrant has suffered substantial physical or mental abuse as a result of having been a victim of certain criminal activity; (2) The immigrant possesses information concerning that criminal activity; (3) The immigrant has been helpful, is being helpful, or is likely to be helpful in the investigation or prosecution of the criminal activity; and (4) The criminal activity described violated the laws of, or occurred in, the United States.

Conclusion

Family violence is a real concern that faces families on a daily basis. Victims can be men or women of any economic class, age, ethnicity, religion, descent, or profession. Not only does family violence affect the victim and his/her family, it also affects the community. As prosecutors, it is our job to help those in need and ensure that people are kept safe. Although not everyone who needs help wants help, it is our job to follow the law and make certain that justice is sought. Family violence is a problem for everyone, not just those for who are physically abused, and we must be aware of that in order to help prevent it.

Quick Reference Guide to Laws

Definition under Texas Family Code, Chapter 71: an act by a member of family or household against another member of family or household that is intended to result in physical harm, bodily injury, assault, or sexual assault or that is a threat that reasonably places the member in fear of imminent physical harm, bodily injury, assault or sexual assault, but does not include defensive measures to protect oneself; abuse of a child be a member of family or household dating violence

Criminal Offenses under Texas Penal Code, various provisions:

Offense	Definition	Punishment
1st Degree Felony	aggravated kidnapping aggravated sexual assault/deadly weapon aggravated sexual assault/ bodily injury burglary of habitation (w/intent to commit a felony) murder	5-99 years OR life OR 2-10 years probation
2nd Degree Felony	aggravated assault/deadly weapon aggravated assault/ serious bodily injury aggravated kidnapping (safe release) burglary of habitation (w/intent to commit theft/assault) sexual assault stalking (2nd)	2-20 years OR 2-10 years probation
3rd Degree Felony	assault bodily injury— enhanced kidnapping retaliation/obstruction stalking unlawful restraint (risk of serious bodily injury) violation of protective order—assault or enhanced	2-10 years OR 2-10 years probation

Misdemeanor—Class A	assault bodily injury criminal trespass interference with emergency call terroristic threat violation of protective order violation of court order/bond in family violence case	up to 1 year in jail OR up to 2 years probation
Misdemeanor—Class B	harassment	up to 180 days in jail OR up to 2 years probation
Misdemeanor—Class C	assault (offensive contact)	fine not to exceed $500

Applicable Definitions for Emergency Protective Orders, Protective Orders:

Protective Order Issue	Applicable Law(s)
Magistrate's Order for Emergency Protection	Art. 17.292 Code of Criminal Procedure
Application for Protective Order	Texas Family Code, Sec. 82.001
Required findings/orders (temporary ex parte PO)	Texas Family Code, Sec. 83.001
Temporary ex parte orders are police enforceable	Texas Penal Code, Sec.25.07(a)
Required findings/orders (final PO)	Texas Family Code, Sec. 85.001

Roshni—North Texas Domestic Violence Program

Serving South Asian, Middle Eastern, and African Immigrants

M. Basheer Ahmed, M.D. and Talaun Thompson, L.M.S.W.

T HE TERMS *DOMESTIC violence, wife beating, battering*, or *family violence* all refer to abuse by one person of another within the context of an intimate relationship. Domestic violence takes on many forms (e.g., physical, emotional, and sexual), but can be best defined as "any behavior that is intended to control and subjugate another human being through the use of fear, humiliation and verbal or physical assault" (Texas Council of Family Violence, 2006). It is often difficult to comprehend that such behavior exists in our society today. But as we will learn, domestic violence is a serious issue that exists in all societies, regardless of religion, culture, economic status, or educational level. The immigrant community is no exception; domestic violence exists within it and has to be addressed.

The Muslim Community Center (MCC) for Human Services has worked hard to fill this need by coordinating volunteers and working with the area's existing services. As we will see, addressing domestic violence within the Muslim community requires a lot more than just a desire to help. Knowledge, organization, coordination, and professional staff members are essential components. Also, the establishment of an organization that specializes in addressing a specific community is vital, even when the primary services designed to address that need are available through already existing mainstream social service agencies.

There are 4 million reported instances of domestic violence every year in the United States. The National Domestic Violence Hotline (NDVH), for example, receives more than 70,000 calls calls for assistance each year. Thirty-one percent of all American women report being physically or sexually abused by their husbands or partners at some point in their lives. Most of these cases go unreported. Women accounted for 39 percent of all hospital emergency department visits for violence-related injuries. More than three women are murdered by their husbands or boyfriends every day in this country. The physical and emotional damage caused by domestic violence costs the nation's medical and mental health system about $4.1 billion each year. (For details, please see *http://ednabuse.org/resources /facts/*.)

Victims of domestic violence can often be described as people who have low self-esteem and a poor self-image and who grew up in a household where they were either abused or neglected. However, regardless of these characteristics, many educated, confident, and intelligent women find themselves as victims. Often the dynamics of the abusive relationship itself can reduce strong women to the level of abject submission. Despite numerous attempts to leave, many women return for a variety of reasons, among them the fear that they or the children will be hurt. In some instances the victims believe that their abusers have really changed, only to learn later that the change was temporary—perhaps just to get them to return home.

Children are often the unintended victims within an abusive household. For example, older siblings are often subjected to violence when they attempt to protect a parent from abuse. In some instances, children are abused because they happen to be at home when the incident occurs. The resulting trauma often results in low self-esteem, depression, poor impulse control, poor academic achievement, and a feeling of powerlessness.

Some people erroneously assume that because the United States and other industrialized countries report such high numbers of abuse, the incident must be a "western" problem. What needs to be understood is that because such countries take domestic abuse seriously, more and more women are able to come forward. This has, consequently, improved the ability of researchers to collect data. In many third world countries (Muslim countries included), where there are no services or support and no means to collect such data, the incident reports will be low.

The late Sharifa Alkhateeb reported that according to a 1993 survey of sixty-three Muslim community workers, leaders, and individuals undertaken by the North American Council for Muslim Women, domestic violence occurred in 10% of the Muslim population. If verbal and psychological abuse were added to this, the figure would rise considerably. As part of her Ph.D. dissertation, Najma M. Adam conducted a study on domestic violence against women within the immigrant and Indo-Pakistani communities in the United States. Nearly 73% of the 61 women interviewed had experienced psychological abuse, 48% had experienced physical abuse, 54%

had experienced sexual abuse, and nearly 39% had sustained abuse-related injuries. Many of the victims were quite reluctant to share information with her. (From papers presented at the first regional conference on Domestic Violence: The Islamic Perspective, February 2001, at University of Texas at Arlington.)

Muslim Community and Domestic Violence.

Countless studies of the Qu'ran, the *hadith*, and the Sunah have shown that Islam does not endorse any type of violence or abuse. Despite the wealth of information, however, the Muslim community appears to engage in such practices that defy Islamic teachings. Some men and women sincerely believe that Islam "justifies" abuse, misinterpret certain Qur'anic verses, and then cite them to excuse their behavior. The use of religion to justify such actions makes it all the more important to involve the community's religious scholars to reeducate and help people eradicate domestic violence within the Muslim household. For families to be healthy and happy, violence and oppression must be eliminated from the community.

Addressing the complex issue of domestic violence has been very challenging for many agencies, including those that have been created by people of South Asia or Arab backgrounds. Efforts intended to provide support, however, are often unorganized and ineffectual. In addition, many victims are reluctant to approach the community due to the fear of gossip or that abusers will become more hostile, a lack of confidence, feelings of hopelessness, financial dependence, and other reasons. In addition, despite the availability of domestic violence shelters and resources within the community, women are reluctant to avail themselves of these services because they are either unaware of them or do not feel comfortable (the service providers might not understand their language, culture, or religion).

Dallas and Tarrant counties are home to 100,000 Muslim immigrants from South Asia, the Middle East, and Africa. They have the same rates of domestic violence as the rest of the population.

Many women fear reporting incidents of domestic violence to the authorities if they are illegal immigrants and thus worry about being deported. Since 9/11, their fears have been and remain quite valid. According to the law, victims of domestic violence can apply for legal status. Uncertainties about legal status, however, can make it all the more difficult for a victim to ask for assistance from a mainstream agency. The availability of a Muslim organization dedicated to domestic violence and related issues could help alleviate some of the fears a person might feel when approaching a mainstream agency. Many abused immigrant women may hesitate to reach out to police, a mainstream shelter, or a domestic violence program due to barriers of language and fear of deportation.

Creating social service programs within a non-profit organization that deals effectively with specific matters might encourage Muslim women to seek help. Numerous studies show that people are more likely to open up and share what is happening to them when they are with a professional who is either similar to them or has a strong understanding of their culture.

The first place that most Muslims turn to for help is the mosque. However, many religious leaders are ill prepared to handle situations involving domestic violence. Despite being well-versed in religion and *fiqh* (Islamic law), they lack the necessary knowledge and expertise as regards domestic violence. Fortunately, here in the Dallas-Fort Worth Metroplex (hereinafter "the Metroplex), religious leaders have been very supportive of all victims of domestic violence, and most of them are knowledgeable about the issue. During October which has been designated "Domestic Violence Month," every year they have spoken out against abusing women and children.

MCC's Domestic Violence Program (Roshni)

MCC is a 501 (c) (3) non-profit organization founded in 1995 by Dr. M. Basheer Ahmed. Dr. Ahmed has served as its executive director since 1995. He supervises the center's medical, social, and educational programs. MCC board of directors consists of professionals holding high administrative positions in such major corporations as American Airlines, Bell Helicopter, Burlington Northern Santa Fe Railway, as well as social and community activists. They help lead the organizations strategic plan, and mission. Members actively participate in monthly meetings, resource sharing and program development.

The MCC was established as a response to the influx of refugees from Iraq, Somalia and Bosnia to the Metroplex. Many newly arrived Muslim families were seeking medical and social services, but were unable to access services due to cultural and language barriers. Community leaders and volunteers organized efforts to create a medical and social program to assist them. MCC serves as a bridge between local services and immigrant communities who are hesitant to seek help. Its objective is to provide primary medical care to immigrants, promote healthy and harmonious family relationships, improve access to services and increase community awareness.

Mission, Vision, and Services

MCC, located in Richland Hills, TX is the only medical and social service charitable organization in the Metroplex dedicated to helping the area's underserved communities deal successfully with the complex challenges created by the duality of culture and lack of appropriate medical and social services. Its long-term vision is to develop a community of people who are thriving and striving to maintain a harmonious family structure by offering counseling and education to prevent marital discord, domestic violence and child abuse. MCC's mission therefore is to provide culturally competent services to victims of domestic violence victims, facilitate social adjustment, and eradicate domestic violence by joining hands with other community agencies that have similar goals. To achieve these goals, the center offers counseling services and plans to open a shelter for the victims of domestic violence.

Al-Shifa Clinic. This is a free medical clinic, which opened in 1998, treats hypertension, diabetes, infections, depression, and other emotional problems found among the Metroplex's indigent residents. Lab tests (provided for a nominal charge), mammograms, prescriptions, ad samples of medicine are also available. Eighteen doctors volunteer their time every weekend morning on rotating basis. Free psychiatric counseling is provided for marital and personal issues, and the eye clinic provides individuals with eyeglass prescriptions, disease and injury screening, prevention education, treatment and referrals. Services are available to all, regardless of religious affiliation or country of origin. In 2008, MCC staff members served 1800 patients at the clinic.

Al-Shifa Women and Children's Clinic.

Some immigrant women are very modest and find it inappropriate to be cared for by male physicians. As a result, a women and children's clinic was established in January 2008 enable female patients to see female physicians. This clinic open every first, second and third Sunday of each month.

An internal survey of MCC clients indicated that the vast majority of women from the immigrant population continue to show a lack of interest in or undervalue the importance of regular breast examinations, and are unaware of the principals of "breast health". Older female immigrants are even more reluctant to consider regular breast examinations due to differences in culture and religion. Many of them have never agreed to a breast examination or allowed themselves to be seen by male doctors. Utilizing a female physician helps women accept information about breast cancer, self-examination, and wellness.

At the Sunday clinic, patients are informed of the importance of scheduling regular mammograms after age 35 or 40 when there is a family history of breast cancer. The husbands of prospective mammogram candidates are also educated about the topic so they can encourage their wives to participate. For qualifying women, MCC arranges free mammogram screenings four times a year in collaboration with community medical agencies.

Helpline

MCC offers a 24-hour helpline that offers callers general assistance for non-emergency calls. Most of the callers who seek medical help are referred to private physicians or to MCC's Al-Shifa Clinic if they do not have insurance. In serious cases, patients are referred to local public hospitals.

Enhancing Relationships

In 1999, Dr. Ahmed founded the Institute of Human Relations to provide premarital, marital, and divorce counseling and education in an attempt to alleviate marital discord and prevent the breakdown of the Muslim family structure. Despite MCC's limited budget, it continues to help young people who were planning to get married recognize the realities of married life and give them an opportunity to openly express their likes, dislikes, preferences, and priorities. Several educational programs have been conducted at various Islamic centers in Dallas, Carrollton, Colleyville, Arlington, and Fort Worth.

Over the past ten years, MCC has established a reputable history in Tarrant County of providing quality premarital and marriage educational programs. Since 2006, its "Healthy Marriage" seminars have helped individuals and couples establish, maintain, and recognize healthy marriages. Four curriculums are used, as appropriate: Prevention and Relationship Enhancement Program (PREP), Couple Communication

(CC), Premarital Interpersonal Choices & Knowledge (PICK), and Active Relationship (AR).

In 2007, there were 14,859 Tarrant County Family violence incidences and the Dallas Police Department Family Violence Unit received approximately 21,000 emergency 911 calls for help due to domestic violence.

The Texas Council on Family Violence (2006) found that 74 percent of all Texans have experienced, or know of a friend, or a family member has experienced some form of domestic violence. Recent reports indicate that the majority of victims of family violence in Texas have been between the ages of 20 and 24. Batterers between the ages of 20 and 24 accounted for the highest number of family violence incidents (Texas Department of Public Safety, 2006). In 2000, the most common weapon involved in family violence cases in Texas was physical force (namely hands, feet, and fists), which accounted for 77 percent of all such incidents. In 2004 116 women were killed by their intimate partners and in 2005, 943,718 women were battered in Texas and received services from various domestic violence programs (Texas Council on Family Violence, 2006).

Special Concerns

As described earlier, immigrant women face problems in seeking help, especially in cases of domestic violence, such as the lack of sufficient resources available to intervene on their behalf when they are confronted with unique cultural and language barriers. Not only is there a need to help these victims of abuse, but the community needs to learn more about the dynamics of domestic abuse among the immigrants.

The Roshni Program: Helping Immigrant Victims of Domestic Violence

In 2001, MCC launched a new program for helping victims of domestic violence. Dr. Basheer Ahmed, along with other community leaders, recognized the need for domestic violence education, advocacy and victim case management. This program began with a one-day regional conference on domestic violence from the Islamic perspective, which was a joint venture sponsored by the School of Social Work, University of Texas at Arlington. In attendance were 150 health care providers and community leaders who had come to listen to Muslim and non-Muslim professionals speak about specific challenges related to domestic violence within immigrant communities.

In the same year, MCC established a hotline and recruited volunteer advocates to answer the calls and refer victims to outpatient counseling. Since 2001, MCC has provided counseling and referral services to the immigrant victims of domestic violence. The organizations major goal is to save the marriage either through counseling or other services but in the case of domestic violence, MCC staff creates a safety plan and helps the victim prepare for separation. Staff members also counsel children who experience trauma in this abusive environment, have established relationships with shelters in the Metroplex area and provide some counseling to the shelters' immigrant residents.

In 2006, MCC received a grant through the Department of Justice and hired a full-time social worker to direct volunteer training. This enabled it to establish Roshni, a more comprehensive program for Victims of domestic violence. Roshni, which means "light" in Urdu, is designed to promote healthy and harmonious family relationships in the South Asian, Middle Eastern and African immigrant communities. We promote the empowerment of women so that they can confront and overcome the cycle of domestic violence and exploitation, help the victims and survivors of domestic abuse improve their access to services, and work to increase community awareness of various forms of violence.

Sara (not her real name) came to the United States from Lebanon after marrying an American citizen. A college graduate who had worked as a lab technician in Lebanon, she did not work after she arrived here. Her husband started abusing her verbally and then physically after they had been married for two years. In the meanwhile, she had a baby and was spending most of the time taking care of the house and the young child. Having no close family members in the country and not having the chance to socialize much and make friends, she only knew a few families whom she had met in the mosque. She heard about Roshni at the mosque and contacted one of its Arabic-speaking volunteers because she was confused, unable to understand her husband's behavior, and did not know her options.

Unwilling to complain to the authorities for fear of being deported and loosing financial support if her husband went to jail, she had been tolerating the abusive behavior out of a feeling of hopelessness. She could not stand on her own feet due to language problems, a lack of driving skills, and, most of all, poor ego-strength and self-confidence. She met the volunteer and, subsequently, the counselor at the mosque. She asked him to come with her to counseling and he refused, in fact the abusive behavior increased after she tried to convince him to come. He was fully aware that she had no place to go and that he was exerting total control over her. Sara continued to receive supportive counseling designed to make her aware of the available options and the struggle she had to go through to become independent.

Aisha (not her real name), another victim of abusive behavior who is from India, called Roshni to complain that she had been living with the extended family. She was spending all of her time cleaning, cooking, and taking care of her husband, three children, and both in-laws. Recently, her father-in-law had become verbally abusive and threatened to slap her if she continued to show "disobedient" behavior. This happened in front of her husband, and she was very upset that he had not intervened. When she asked him about his lack of involvement, he explained that he could not ask his father to change his behavior and that she would have to adjust to the situation. She was very apprehensive and depressed due to her husband's lack of support and humiliating behavior. Luckily, in this case the husband was willing to come in for counseling and the couple was eventually referred to family counseling by a professional.

Mrs. Janib (not her real name), a young women in her 30s, reluctantly called Roshni after tolerating several years of emotional and physical abuse by her husband. During the early years of her marriage, she used to discourage other women for blaming their husbands and in-laws. When her own husband started abusing her, she became a silent, submissive victim due to her strong religious conviction that she should submit and obey her husband. When the abusive behavior increased over the next several years and he threatened to divorce her, she knew that she would miss him and become afraid of starting a new life. She had no self-confidence and became hopeless. After calling Roshni for help, she came in for counseling several times before gaining the self-confidence to manage her life on her own. Before filing for divorce, she got a job in a department store and learned of the public services to which she is entitled, such as Section 8 housing, food stamps, and insurance coverage for her six-year-old daughter. The religious background of the staff member helping her, consultation with the Imam, and the counseling sessions helped her make this progress.

Roshni provides community education, culture-sensitive peer counseling, professional counseling, case management, client advocacy, information on women's rights, how to seek help from other service providers, and victim compensation. MCC also provides referrals for legal services and to shelter, and helps victims develop a safety plan. Since its inception in 2006, Roshni has disseminated information about domestic violence and discussed related issues in mosques, community centers, and other places. Women have been encouraged to share if they experience such problems or if they know other women who are experiencing a similar situation. The program has also encouraged women to seek help by distributing pamphlets and brochures, having small woman-only sessions, and holding seminars at various locations on this subject.

Since September 2006, Roshni has trained volunteers how to respond to calls regarding domestic violence issues in a confidential and professional manner, give appropriate advice, and encourage the individual or family to seek counseling (which may help during the early stages of a dispute). The telephone has a messaging service that allows the caller to provide a safe time and telephone number for a volunteer to call and talk with her one-on-one. In situations that are more serious, volunteers have been trained to help the victim find a domestic violence shelter in her local community, arrange transportation, and meet her at the shelter to relieve some of the anticipated stress and anxiety.

Direct Services

Roshni offers a variety of services, including crisis intervention, support, counseling; and referrals to legal services, housing agencies, health and human services, medical and psychiatric services, and shelter for abused women. Its fourteen volunteers have completed forty hours of training in crisis intervention, safety planning, signs of abuse, hotline, confidentiality, available resources, and knowledge of other local and national agencies doing similar work. Most of the volunteers are are from South Asia and the Middle East, and thus are familiar with the various ethnic communities' culture and languages. In addition, they are supervised and receive ongoing training from three full-time staff members, two master-level social workers and one outreach coordinator. For many victims of domestic violence, talking with volunteers provides a great source of relief and hope. Volunteers discuss crisis intervention techniques with staff members and make appropriate recommendations to the client. Staff members also discuss a variety of issues with each client directly, as needed.

Counseling

The majority of immigrant victims dread separation and divorce. In spite of living in an abusive relationship for many years, they do not wish to discuss such options due to the fear of isolation, lack of support, poor skills, a lack of the self-confidence needed to be independent, and some cultural and religious constraints. Many victims need counseling in order to acquire a clear understanding of the dynamics of abuse and how an abusive environment affects their children. On many occasions, clients have to be referred to religious counseling and staff members have to work closely with the client and the community's religious leaders.

Professional counselors offer marital counseling, but usually this approach does not improve the situation. Many perpetrators refuse to participate, and even when they do they show a domineering attitude. As a result, clients are generally hesitant to express their feelings and share there experiences due to the fear of reprisal. Many victims do not get support from family members, and some religious leaders advise them to be patient and obedient. The major focus of counseling through Roshni is to prepare victims to take action and protect themselves and the children from the abusive environment.

The Need for a Separate Shelter

Many South Asian, African and Middle Eastern immigrant women have barriers that may keep them from seeking the safety of a shelter. As a result, they may continue to suffer or, at worst, be killed by their husbands. Domestic violence is a serious issue, and many of its victims need mental health, legal, and support services. Without creating an environment of trust and familiarity, individuals may hesitate to take advantage of the available services. Many immigrant women are modest and do not outwardly challenge the various discomforts experienced in American domestic violence shelters.

Language and cultural issues may pose the most obvious barriers to services; however, there are also religious issues that may not be easily detected. For example, food and its preparation are important factors that must be understood and respected. Also prayer, fasting, and other rituals, along with taking care of children, the relationship with family, and other factors, all must be taken into consideration when creating an environment in which the client can be comfortable and can trust. MCC, which has wanted to establish a domestic violence shelter for Muslim women for many years, understands the impact that such a place could have in the lives of women who are currently suffering.

MCC is currently seeking funds to establish a separate shelter for South Asian, African, and Middle Eastern immigrant women. At the present time, it is using the existing facility of the Mosaic family program and shelter in Dallas, the only multi-cultural family violence program in the city that serves refugees and immigrants. This program assists immigrants, refugees, asylums seekers, victims of trafficking who experience psychological problems, and victims of domestic violence. Mosaic staff members speak various languages and are familiar with their clients' cultural uniqueness. Roshni staff members work closely with their Mosaic counterparts and at times collaborate to assist victims.

Funding

Funding remains a challenging issue. Developing a self-sufficient center, however, requires fundraising. Since 1995, MCC has hosted an annual fundraising dinner. Fundraising initiatives have been organized by contacting local physicians and businesspeople by mail for donations and contacting local Muslim organizations and mosques to support special projects. The center receives some corporate funds, namely, those that are donated by Muslim employees of those corporations. In addition, a small Susan G. Komen Foundation grant supports the breast cancer outreach education program, the Harris Methodist Health Foundation provided a small education and marketing grant for the MCC-Roshni Domestic Violence program, and the Department of Justice allowed the center to hire a volunteer coordinator and develop a volunteer training program. Islamic centers and mosques also give some financial support, but since MCC has to compete with many other charitable organizations and mosques, it is extremely difficult to secure enough donations. Currently, the organization is raising funds in the community to continue its domestic violence programs and is seeking additional grant money for its envisaged shelter.

MCC has attracted national attention, and a prototype has been replicated in other cities. The need to make adequate and appropriate medical care, social services, and education awareness available to the Metroplex's underserved communities is immense. The barriers experienced by immigrants who need help are overwhelming. MCC has therefore positioned itself to become a model program for providing comprehensive medical and social services to immigrant communities.

References

Texas Council of Family Violence (2006). *Domestic violence report.* Retrieved on May 27, 2008 from *www.tcfv.org*

Texas Department of Public Safety (2006). Crime in Texas: Family Violence. Retrieved on April 5, 2008 from *http://www.txdps.state.tx.us/ crimereports/07/citch5.pdf*

Resource for additional information: *www.mcc-hs.org*

LaVergne, TN USA
20 September 2009
158406LV00003B/2/P